BUGATTI VEYRON
A QUEST FOR PERFECTION

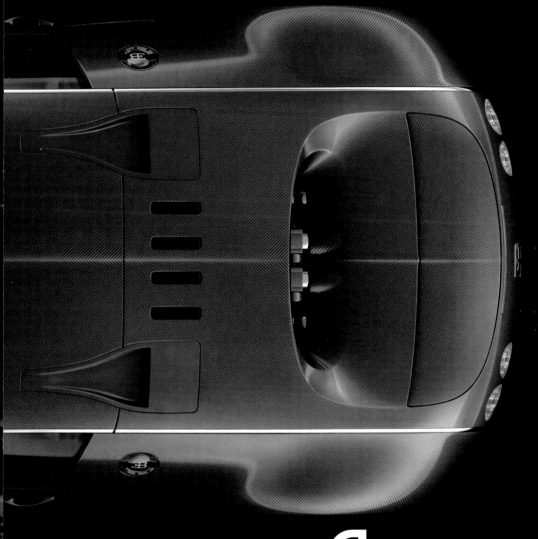

BUGATTI VEYRON

A QUEST FOR PERFECTION

Martin Roach

ρ

preface
publishing

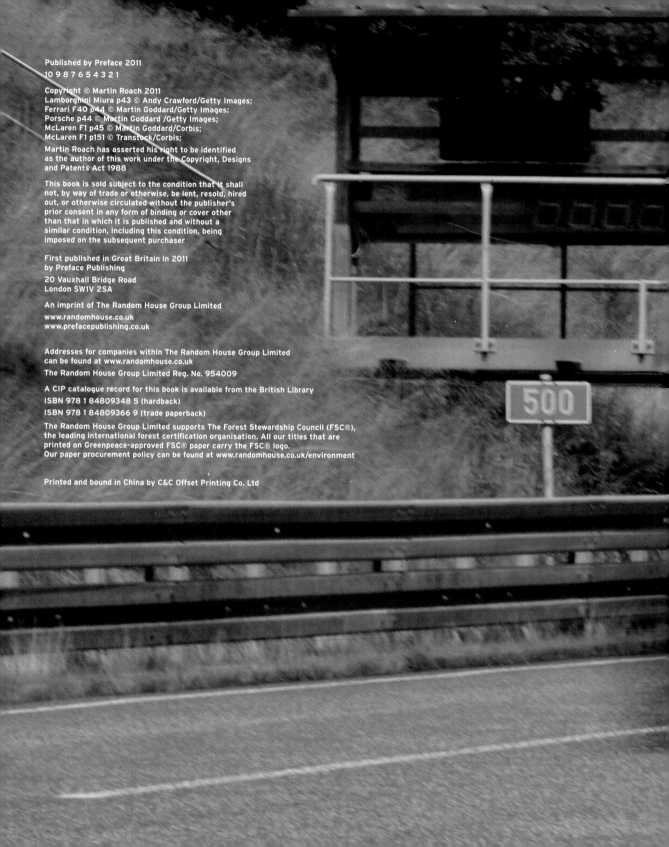

Published by Preface 2011

10 9 8 7 6 5 4 3 2 1

First published in Great Britain in 2011
by Preface Publishing

20 Vauxhall Bridge Road
London SW1V 2SA

An imprint of The Random House Group Limited

www.randomhouse.co.uk
www.prefacepublishing.co.uk

Addresses for companies within The Random House Group Limited
can be found at www.randomhouse.co.uk

The Random House Group Limited Reg. No. 954009

A CIP catalogue record for this book is available from the British Library

ISBN 978 1 84809348 5 (hardback)

ISBN 978 1 84809366 9 (trade paperback)

The Random House Group Limited supports The Forest Stewardship Council (FSC®),
the leading international forest certification organisation. All our titles that are
printed on Greenpeace-approved FSC® paper carry the FSC® logo.
Our paper procurement policy can be found at www.randomhouse.co.uk/environment

Printed and bound in China by C&C Offset Printing Co. Ltd

CONTENTS

INTRODUCTION

I began this book on a sunny day in London's Mayfair, in the summer of 2010. Enjoying a family break in the capital, we were on our way to Ripley's Believe It Or Not Museum, a vast building in the centre of Piccadilly crammed with impossible creations, waxworks, objets d'art and other ephemera of the peculiar. On our way from the hotel, we turned a sharp left into a one-way system near Bond Street and that's when I saw it . . .

A gleaming white Bugatti Veyron Grand Sport.

Parked up on the left, clutching the road as if it were about to start eating the tarmac.

'Oh my God, look at that!' I shouted to my two boys in the back. I swerved a little too hastily and parked my own (somewhat less gleaming) car on a double yellow line. 'Come on, boys, let's go and have a look'. Bemused but not surprised, my wife chuckled as we jumped out.

As we walked over to the Veyron, I noticed the driver was still in the car, on his phone (yes, he'd pulled over to make the call). He was casually dressed and looked impossibly rich. I vividly remember the extravagantly chunky watch on his tanned left wrist, a timepiece that also looked impossibly expensive. The car's number plate was just two digits, I suspect worth more than many people's houses and certainly worth more than most people's cars. I chaperoned my two boys to the front of the vehicle, camera in hand, then caught the driver's eye with a slight nod of my head and lifted my eyebrows, asking his permission to take a photo. He smiled warmly and nodded back. So I positioned my boys at the nose of the Veyron and quickly, nervously, took a snap. That's when I noticed that my heart was beating really fast and I was slightly short of breath. I had goosebumps too.

As we gazed longingly at the Veyron – like pretty much everyone else walking down the street that day – I started to realise that on seeing the revolutionary Bugatti, I felt exactly the same way that I do when I come across a big celebrity. That sense of 'Am I really seeing this?', a childlike wonder that sweeps over you whenever you stumble across a famous face or high-profile person that you admire.

As a ghostwriter, I am fortunate enough to come into contact with celebrities as a daily part of my job, and yet one of the most joyful aspects of making my living in this mysterious and unusual way is that the enjoyment just doesn't wear off. Over the course of a book project, you inevitably become quite close to your famous subject, who has usually spent many weeks or maybe months revealing their lives and innermost secrets to you. And during that time, as their ghost, you inevitably become very relaxed with them in return, such intimacy is a necessarily reciprocal but very pleasant part of the complex process. Yet on many occasions I am still caught short by their celebrity, perhaps when an excited fan comes over for an autograph, or maybe there's an unexpected clip on TV when I'm back at home eating dinner with the kids. It's not just because I'm a ghost either, we've all had the same feeling when we have spotted someone famous in a crowd, maybe at a football match, in a shopping mall, a restaurant or perhaps on holiday. That's when we get that feeling.

And that day in Mayfair I felt the same way. That's when I realised . . . this car, the Bugatti Veyron, essentially a chunk of metal on four circles of rubber, has become a bona-fide post-modern *celebrity*.

As an unashamed petrolhead, I knew all about the Veyron, of course. I knew (some of) the mind-boggling statistics; I knew about the innovative and courageous thinking behind the concept of the world's fastest road car; I had seen the TV shows, read the many press reviews. But that afternoon, having witnessed this modern marvel in the flesh and been taken aback by my visceral reaction to it, I decided that there was something more to this machine than just a triumph of engineering. There was something intangible, something I had to find out about . . .

So I got to wondering if I could 'ghost' the Veyron. Or at least tell its tale through the eyes and minds of the people who were behind its genesis. If this was, after all, a modern-day celebrity, then it had a story to tell, secrets to reveal. Of course, even Bugatti haven't equipped their masterpiece with artificial intelligence that would allow me to interview it (we'll leave that to Hasselhoff's KITT for now), but the premise was an intriguing one: could I tell the car's tale, through the people, the voices, the minds and motives of those who produced it?

To do this, I would have to get close to the Bugatti. Very close, just as I would when working with a celebrity. I'd have to see it in private quarters, surrounded by those familiar to its everyday life; see how it came to exist as a celebrity today; unearth what thinking, dedication and ambition went into that success. And, of course, I'd need to drive one. Without a drive in this mythical beast, my quest would merely be a biography, a distant third-party opinion on a famous car.

I was once asked by a world-famous pop group to join them on stage in front of 18,000 people 'to feel exactly what it is like to be in this band'. I sat for over an hour next to the keyboard player while the thousands of fans in front of me must have wondered who on earth the hooded figure crouched on stage was. In terms of understanding exactly what it takes to be in a huge band and stand in front of a cavernous arena filled with screaming fans, that invite was brilliantly successful and left me in no uncertain terms as to what that life is like. And driving the Veyron would be the automotive equivalent. I'd need to spend time with the subject of the book itself. And see life through those eyes.

So I set out on this quest. Remember that Veyron owner's watch? Like its owner, that glittering time-piece looked 'impossibly' expensive. It's a word that is synonymous with the Veyron: impossible ambition, impossible speed, power, torque, exclusivity, precision, acceleration etc. But it's not impossible is it? It was sitting there on that side street in Mayfair. The Veyron was Bugatti's quest for perfection; and now I had to start on my own quest, a journey to discover how they achieved this 'impossible' feat: who was behind it, how they made it, what it is like to own one, and also why we are so fascinated by such cars. To see this car in person is an unexpurgated joy, one that I'd been lucky enough to experience before I put pen to paper; but to drive this millionaire's car would be my own impossible quest.

It was a quest which would take me flying across the Channel to a town named 'Car City', then driving through the mountainous Alsace region to a little village where they assemble this remarkable vehicle. I'd also slip into a supercar bunker in west London and finally people watch in Monaco, the opulent anti-ghetto in southern France brimming with multimillionaires. Along the way I would talk to engineers, drivers, historians, and the ultra-wealthy; it quickly became apparent this was a story as much about *people* as it was about a car.

One caveat to the tale is that I am not a motoring journalist and so I will not be peppering these pages with technical minutiae, such as my own opinions of the complex relationship between the Veyron's con-rods and disc-brake chambers. This car, perhaps more than any other in the modern era, has been written about with great expertise and insight by a motoring media that are paid to be critical and objective, a hard-nosed bunch of experts whose intimate knowledge of thousands of cars never ceases to amaze me. That expertise has never been more apparent than in their well-documented writing about the Veyron.

So I doff my cap to this vast wealth of writers who have produced magazine articles about the Veyron and I do not pretend to compete in that particular technical arena (I have kept the more technical data for captions). Yet even these writers seem to fall under the spell of the Bugatti's overpowering and beguiling charms.

This is a more personal quest. To tell the car's story and ultimately to drive a Bugatti Veyron. I hope that by telling the tale of the car, through the words and experiences of the people who designed it, engineered it, tested and made it, but also through the opinions of those who own it, love it, review it and even a few who dislike it, this incredible modern crusade will become a little clearer.

CHAPTER ONE
THE CELEBRITY

Before I can attempt to 'meet' the subject in question, I need to look at the enigma that is the Bugatti Veyron and to present an introductory potted history of the car that became a celebrity. By the time I'd decided to write this book, the Veyron's celebrity was already well established, having fascinated the car-loving public and motoring world for over ten years. But exactly what do I mean by a 'celebrity'?

The definition of a celebrity is a highly subjective notion. Tracing back the etymological roots of the word offers up a derivation from the Latin 'celebratatum', meaning 'the condition of being famous', although this word can also mean 'populous' or 'crowded'. This rather imprecise start aside, there are certain (X) factors which most people would acknowledge qualify someone – or something – as being a celebrity. A degree of fame is essential, but this usually needs to reach beyond a specific niche and into a broader sphere, a two-tier level of fame that exists in the wider mainstream. The celebrity often – although not always – has achieved something of note or been recognised for an accomplishment. There is often an element of money that is beyond most 'ordinary' people (again this is not exclusively the case). Further, a celebrity will often have a 'subculture' surrounding them that is obsessive, fascinated and adoring. And, finally, as I know from many years of working with celebrities, there is undeniably an unquantifiable 'something extra' which sets the subjects of our fascination apart from their contemporaries. It's also true that even when many of these elements are present, celebrity is still a very subjective term; one person's hero is another's nobody. Similarly, certain celebrities have a degree of aura projected on to them by a public avidly wanting to see and meet them. This can sometimes inflate their 'presence' beyond what it is in actuality.

Not so the Veyron. Its reputation goes before it. The Bugatti certainly ticks most if not all of these 'celebrity' boxes. Firstly, it is beyond doubt that the car had achieved a level of notoriety and fame within the automotive industry even before its long-awaited media launch in 2005. We'll come to that prolonged gestation later, but for now, in order to look at the extent of the car's celebrity within its own niche, let's examine the 'headlines' for the vehicle itself.

On its much-anticipated launch, the Bugatti Veyron stunned the motoring world. Named after the revered Bugatti race driver and 1939 Le Mans winner,

Pierre Veyron, the car's performance figures were indeed guaranteed to grab headlines: an unprecedented 1001bhp engine, a 0–60 time of just 2.5 seconds, a top speed of 253mph and a launch day price tag of £810,345. The launch event for journalists was in mid-October 2005 in the mountainous Madonie region in Sicily, where the fortunate few were helicoptered in and invited to blast the machine around the beautiful setting for the famous Targa Florio road race. But exactly why were the press so bowled over? To find that out, let's break the celebrity down into its basic component parts, and to do that we have to spend a little time getting our hands oily.

First up, that monstrous engine. The Veyron boasts the most powerful engine ever put into a road car, the so-called W16. It is an 8-litre engine that generates a mythical – and still largely unrivalled – 1001bhp. To put that into context, the blistering 2010 Ferrari 458 model has 560bhp, almost half; the previous fastest car in the world, the beautiful McLaren F1 had 627bhp; the Veyron's 1001bhp is around ten times that of a normal road car (of course, it's important to note the overriding importance of a car's so-called 'power-to-weight ratio', which in both the F1 and 458 are prodigiously strong; the Veyron is a substantially heavier

Using a conventional V8 engine with 16 litres would be too big and would require huge pistons which would not be able to revolve at the 6000rpm needed. Some observers have suggested you'd actually need a 48-litre V8, in which case you'd also need a car the size of several buses to fit it all in!

vehicle. The comparisons given here are purely in terms of bhp and designed merely to highlight the extremity of the 1001 bhp figure.)

To generate 1001bhp, it was calculated that the equivalent of two large V8 engines would be needed. Simply welding two V8s next to each other or even in a straight line would have produced an engine too big to fit into a car. The solution was to rest two VR8 'engines' (a concept originated in the VW group) together in the shape of the letter 'W', hence the name. They shared a crankshaft which completed the remarkable melding together; so the W16 engine is essentially two V8 engines strapped together.

This massively powerful engine is ably assisted by no fewer than four turbochargers. The power boost this generates for the engine is huge. Many supercars boast one turbo, some two, but four is exceptional, with only one precedent (itself an earlier Bugatti). All of this power creates a ludicrous amount of heat so the car was fitted with *ten* radiators. By doubling the amount of cylinders and turbocharging the engine too, Bugatti had produced an engine that, frankly, could melt a volcano. That achievement in itself was front-page stuff.

At 710 millimetres in length, the Veyron's 16-cylinder mid-engine is not necessarily bigger than a conventional V12 power unit. Its compact dimensions are made possible by the unique W layout, made up of two offset double row banks, each comprising eight cylinders and with a bank angle of 15 degrees.

The two banks in the W16 are set at an angle of 90 degrees to each other, housed in a single crankcase meaning they function as a single engine, in this instance aspirated by four turbochargers.

The engine has four valves per cylinder, 64 valves in total. It has a dry-sump lubrication system influenced by Formula 1 technology and innovative engine cooling systems.

The engine is 71cm long and weighs around 400kg. Maximum torque is a frankly bonkers 1250Nm (922ft/lb).

So Bugatti had created an engine for a road car that possessed more bhp and acceleration than a Nascar. Clearly, generating such colossal power was all very impressive but if the gearbox fitted was remotely ordinary, the amount of energy passing through the transmission would shatter the teeth on the gears in milliseconds. Something completely unique had to be created to harness this apocalyptic power. The new car would boast an engine torque of 1250 Newton metres (Nm), which was staggering. So, like much of the Veyron, the gearbox became a case of 'reinventing the wheel' (if you will excuse the pun) that saw Bugatti fit the Veyron with a so-called 'DSG box'. For the gearbox anoraks among you, that is a 'seven-speed direct-shift gearbox, computer-controlled sequential and manual gearbox accessed via a super-fast dual clutch'. VW evolved an idea that had been used previously within their group from 2003 in a simpler form for cars such as the Golf R32 and a little later the Audi TT.

A conventional car uses a single clutch to prepare the next gear. But the Veyron has two clutches, so, for example, while you are driving along in fourth gear, the second clutch will prepare fifth gear, ready and waiting for an almost instant gear change. In fact, the car's gear changing is so swift as to be virtually

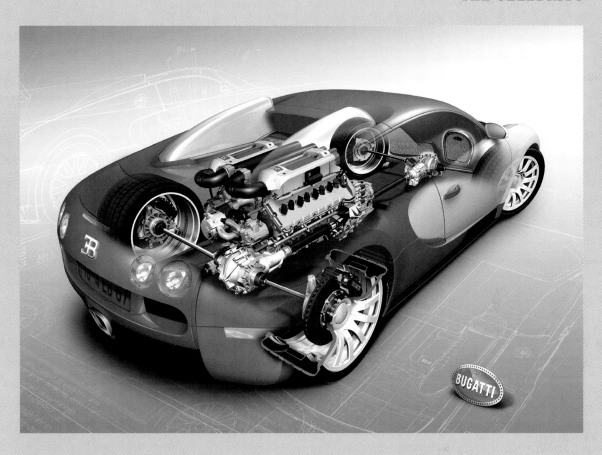

instant, resulting in a negligible loss of acceleration. And this system could be operated by the driver in either an automatic or manual mode. The lightning-quick gear changes offered by the Veyron's 'dual clutch' configuration are extraordinary even in the context of supercar history.

The whole complex set-up is controlled by computers akin to those used in F1; there is no clutch pedal as these computers control the clutch discs as well as the actual gear shifting. For the Veyron, Bugatti wanted this ultra-complex gearbox system to achieve all of these remarkable feats *reliably* – similar technology on an F1 car is designed to sometimes last only a few hours; the Veyron gearbox was expected to last at least ten years, ideally many more. A team of fifty engineers spent five years perfecting the system. Two engineers build just one gearbox a week. Yet more headlines.

Once Bugatti had the enormous 1001bhp harnessed through that highly innovative gearbox, the distribution of all this power to the road had to be via permanent four-wheel drive – otherwise the car would most likely just suffer almost constant wheel spin. And the Veyron's four wheels were themselves gargantuan, the rear tyres being the biggest ever fitted to a road car. This meant

The Veyron is a so-called 'mid-engine' supercar, a layout which is very useful for favourable weight distribution. The heaviest part of the car is thus near the centre of the vehicle, which is better for holding and also overall balance and stability. The rear tyres have more weight above them so therefore more traction too. One obvious drawback – almost always no rear seats.

The mythical 1001bhp gauge in the 16.4 Veyron.

that the Kwik-Fit Price Promise was never going to work so Bugatti commissioned Michelin to create a tyre unique to the Veyron. The aim was for a perfect mix between a slick, grippy race tyre and one that could cope with the vagaries of a public road but also last an acceptable amount of time so as to be practical.

Of course, it's no use having such phenomenal power and grip if the car is shaped like a box. So aerodynamics were crucial to the Veyron. Although it is relatively heavy for this type of super sports car, the Veyron is not overly large: 2 metres wide, 4.47 metres long and only 1.22 metres high. This is very wide in proportion to its height, hence the car's striking and powerful squat appearance.

Although VW engineers were the driving force behind the project, there were certain areas of development where it was deemed necessary to bring in specialist skills. In 2000 Bristol-based Ricardo was selected by Bugatti as the engineering partner for the complete transmission and driveline system. As well as the actual mechanical system design itself, Ricardo were also involved in 'the design and development of the complex mechatronic system which controls the 7-speed Dual Clutch Transmission as well as all the active 4WD driveline units including all new algorithm and software development and control unit design'. The partnership didn't stop there – so innovative and unprecedented was this car that even the testing facilities, factory and almost every aspect of the project had to be bespoke, so Ricardo were also intimately involved in developing the technology demonstrator.

You've probably guessed by now that this is not a Haynes Manual, and the above mechanical basics will only ever *really* interest those with a particular interest in automotive engineering. What this basic summary explains, however, is why the Bugatti Veyron's arrival caused such a stir in the motoring press – and hence its immediate niche celebrity.

However, what created even more headlines and a high profile was what all this engineering technology meant in terms of performance. The years of innovation produced a set of performance statistics that frankly *shocked* the motoring world – guaranteeing the Veyron's overnight celebrity status. The fabled 0–60mph time is indeed just 2.5 seconds, assisted by a lunatic launch-control system taken from Formula 1. To put that into everyday context, if the Veyron took off from a football pitch's goal line, it would hit 60mph before the centre circle.

And as the speeds go up, the Veyron's performance seems to get even more crazy: the car has a 0–100–0mph time of 9.9sec. This braking would create more g-force than the pilot of an F-16 jet fighter would experience at take-off. If you wanted to get to 100mph, you'd only need 462 feet, only 50 feet more than the football pitch. Top speed is the aforementioned 253mph, the fastest of all time for a road car. At that velocity, the car is covering the entire length of the same football pitch *per second*; to test the car from 0 to 250 and back to 0 again, you would need a three-mile straight.

That top speed of 253mph is almost a third of the speed of sound, yet it can be reached in less than a minute. At that velocity, the car will run out of

The Veyron's brakes are a huge 400mm diameter (front) and 380mm (rear), with 8 and 6 (titanium) piston racing calipers respectively, a spec taken from the aerospace industry.

fuel from its 100-litre tank in just twelve minutes, covering only 51 miles. That's around 2.3 miles per gallon. At that point it would be sucking in air at a rate of 45,000 litres a minute, as much as a human being breathes in four days. With the Veyron's fuel tank pumping petrol in eight times faster than a normal car, Bugatti needed yet another bespoke solution: a tank with 250 parts that took three days just to weld.

But there were other, less obvious, 'headline' figures that were equally compelling: the car is not just impressive in the sprint. The Veyron can brake faster than it can accelerate, so it will get back from 60mph to zero in just 2.2 seconds (The brakes' power is far greater than even the prodigious W16 engine – the equivalent of 4000bhp). Extrapolating that deceleration out means that its time for 0–60 and then back to 0 is in theory just 4.7 seconds, the same time it

takes some Porsche 911 Carreras to get to 60mph. To go back to my football-pitch analogy, if a Veyron flies past the goal post at 60mph, it will come to a complete standstill just 31 metres later, halfway between the penalty box and the centre circle. If you find yourself in the unenviable position of achieving its top speed and then needing to make an emergency stop, the Veyron can come to a complete standstill from 253mph in just ten seconds. You'll need half a kilometre to do that and your dinner will most likely come up, but nonetheless, those are the facts.

To help stop the car from such a prodigious speed, Bugatti fitted the Veyron with humongous carbon-ceramic brakes, among the largest ever fitted to a road car. But it still needed even more stopping power, so an air brake was built into the rear of the car. This morphing rear wing worked in partnership with an

adjustable suspension that would move up or down depending on the speeds the car was travelling, thus generating more downforce as required. The rear wing did this automatically, in other words *almost by instinct*. The light-speed sensor technology in this rear wing was taken largely from the aerospace industry, very similar in fact to the method used to raise the flaps on aircraft. Which is just as well, because at its top speed, a Veyron is travelling faster than Concorde on take-off. A plane in all but name, then.

Any crash at such crazy speeds would obviously be proportionately more serious. So the Veyron was fitted with a Formula 1-inspired carbon-fibre monocoque for the driver's cabin, which made it one of the strongest cars ever built, scoring maximum points in crash tests (there are airbags too). This technology had been used before on cars such as the Porsche Carrera GT, and even the Audi S4 had carbon trim pieces, but on the Veyron the principle was taken to new extremes of super-strength.

And yet, despite all these record-breaking figures, perhaps the biggest slice of 'X factor' which the car possessed was the remarkable fact that the Bugatti Veyron was very easy to drive around town or to the shops, even. By *anyone*. And that price tag of £810,345 . . . another record beater.

So the Veyron is the fastest road car ever, the most powerful, it has the biggest tyres, a uniquely fast gearbox, it's the most expensive and could be driven by your granny . . . It's plain to see why it caused such a stir in a motoring media that was accustomed to using superlatives. One thing was for certain: within the supercar niche, its celebrity was assured.

Cynics will point out no doubt that other supercars also enjoy such celebrity within the motoring world. That's very true, of course, but one very striking aspect of the Veyron – the characteristic which more than any other drew me to write about it – is the degree of celebrity it enjoys *outside* its specialist niche of motor cars. No other car I've read about and enthused over has the level of profile that a Bugatti Veyron enjoys.

The actual process of writing this book itself has proven this fact beyond doubt. Usually, when I begin a new ghost job, my friends, family and neighbours will ask who I am working with. Sometimes most people will have heard of the celebrity in question, other times it's someone more specialist. Further, even if they recognise the name, the subject of the ghost is not necessarily one that everybody will enthuse about.

Not so the Veyron. I think with one exception ('a Bugatti what?'), *every* person I told about this book not only knew of the car but also clearly hankered after it. My petrolhead property developer friend was a sure bet, of course, but I'd not expected the same reaction from my neighbour in his sixties, nor the

The technology for the light-speed sensors built into the rear wing is measured in piquoseconds – a thousand-billionth of a second. This is the fastest part of any Veyron and is installed by Heggemann Aerospace, who also had to make a bespoke testing machine for the wing's development.

In normal driving, the rear wing is retracted; at 135mph it rises to 15 degrees. Over 230mph it retracts to just two degrees; for high-speed stops it hits 55 degrees in 0.4 seconds.

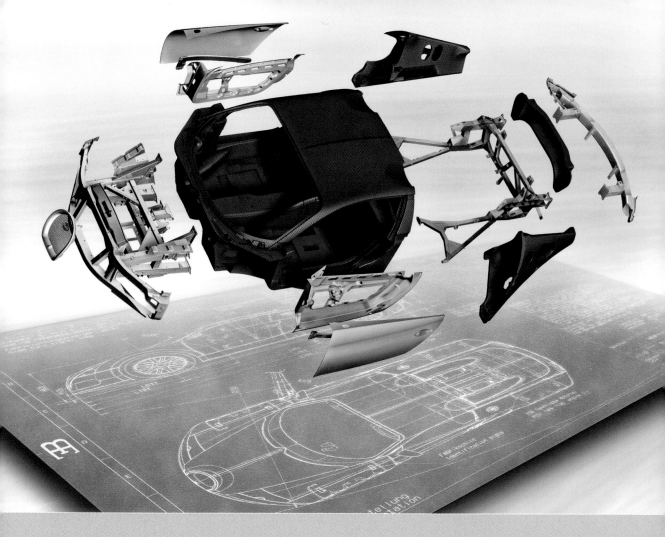

several mums down the school playground who went glassy-eyed at the news. Never before have so many people offered to 'hold my bag' or 'do the research'. The phrase 'household name' is a convenient cliché, but that's what the Veyron's widespread celebrity represents.

Digging deeper, *true* celebrities also have their own fanatical following. A blacked-out people carrier I was once travelling in with a pop star was tailed by a convoy of ten cars from Birmingham to Plymouth, filled with fans waving, taking photos, winding windows down to shout across the carriageway. Ditto the Veyron.

How do I know this? Because the car is papped like a celebrity; if a Veyron crashes, races along the Autobahn at breakneck speeds, gets a parking ticket or is even just spotted in a street, you can rest assured that within hours there is a YouTube clip posted online. Just type in 'Veyron+Autobahn' or 'Veyron+crash' or 'Veyron+getting ticket'. The most famous clip is perhaps the one showing a Veyron crashing and plunging into a salt water lagoon in America. After the footage lit up the internet for some days, it was suggested that the crash was the result of the driver swerving to avoid a pelican; within hours, internet pranksters put a can of pelican repellent for sale on an auction website for $2 million.

On another photo website, a picture of a Slovakian Veyron in a wheel clamp was posted within hours of the event. Likewise there's a photo of a Veyron in London with a ticket on the windscreen and another of a car in Las Vegas that had run out of gas. There's also footage of a bump on a test drive (hopefully not one that was run on a 'you crash it, you fix it' basis). There are also online reports of a Bugatti smashing into a cactus and another story where a relative of the owner pranged it. At the time of writing, YouTube lists 43,000 results for 'Veyron'.

Google 'Bugatti vs Ferrari street race' and you'll see what happened when those two cars decided to square up to one another in the company of a rather ill-equipped BMW police car. There are also pictures of the supposed first ever crash of a Veyron on a public road (in the UK, due to aquaplaning, apparently) and other such landmarks. And, just as I did on that summer's day in Mayfair, many of these 'paps' feel they have to first ask *permission* to take photographs of the car.

It's not just exciting footage or photographs, either. Similarly there are chat rooms dedicated to the car; there's even an unofficial Facebook page. A social network page . . . about a car.

It isn't just the web, either. The car mags are understandably filled with reviews, and TV took the lead too. Most famously, we've all seen James May on *Top Gear* taking the Super Sport version of the Veyron to 259mph – at the time a world record for a production car – only for Bugatti's test driver Pierre-Henri Raphanel to top him with 267.856mph a few moments later. No corner of the media seems exempt from the Veyron's celebrity.

Like all big celebrities, the car has a dedicated fan base. There are only 450 coupes and convertible Veyrons in total, but the car's following is not limited to these lucky few owners. It has a global following, in my personal experience *exactly* akin to that of a pop star, sportsman or other celebrity. And, again like other celebrities, this one also has celebrity fans. Beyoncé Knowles is rumoured to have bought her husband Jay-Z a convertible Veyron Grand Sport for his forty-first birthday (mind you, for Beyoncé's twenty-ninth birthday, he had bought her an island).

Celebrities have associated merchandise around them too. If you are lucky enough to be able to afford the Veyron but still want a model for your mantelpiece, how about a solid-gold replica, shaped entirely out of 24-carat gold and encrusted with 7.2 carats' worth of diamonds? This 'ornament' is made by Robert Gulpen of Munich & Stuart Hughes in Liverpool, and any one of the limited edition of three will cost a reported £2 million. More than your standard Veyron, even. Not exactly a Tonka toy.

For those of you with slightly less hefty wallets, there's always a high-end scale replica, although this will still set you back nearly £3500. Italian pen-maker Ferrari da Varese has worked with Bugatti to design a very exclusive pen said to be inspired by the Bugatti Veyron. The 'Bugatti Type A' pen is designed by Luigi Trenti, crafted from aluminium and plated in nickel, then sterling silver, then palladium and finally platinum. The nib is made from 18-carat gold, and comes complete with a sapphire glass window and a black embossed Bugatti logo. It's £15,000. I'm saving as we speak. I could also buy (in theory) a Bugatti vault for €60,000, a Bugatti watch for €150,000, an ornamental decanter styled after the radiator grille and various other Bugatti-inspired pens and perfumes. One German company has even taken the engine block and turned it into a $75,000 watch winder. I think I'll get a baseball cap.

If that's still too pricey, maybe copy some students from Xian University in China who made a Veyron out of 10,280 empty cigarette packets. It weighed 660lb and was even powered by its own electric motor. It was supposed to raise awareness for World Smoking Day but perhaps also helped the cause 'Students With Nothing Better To Do Day'.

If you think smoking your way through over 200,000 cigarettes is a daft way to pay homage to the great car, you could always copy a man called Sheepo who cleverly built a Veyron out of Lego Technic pieces. This included a remote-controlled braking system, a powered targa roof and motorised rear spoiler. Even the gear lever moved and the car could reverse. All of these entertaining and unusual fan gestures are the exact same personal homages that rock stars, sports stars and TV celebrities enjoy.

So the Veyron clearly enjoys a massive following within the motor industry; it also has a far more widespread profile among the general public; its technical and performance achievements reinforce this profile and the financial figures surrounding it are not exactly 'normal'; the end result is that the car has its own fan base who would testify that the Veyron does, indeed, have the 'X factor'.

So for all of these reasons, in my mind the Bugatti Veyron is a bona-fide celebrity and therefore it became the next logical 'famous face' that I wanted to write about. As with any celebrity I work with, by definition I need to tell the tale of their incarnation, achievements, impact, the genius behind their fame, the *people* behind them. The question was, would I be able to meet this celebrity? And most importantly of all, would I get to drive it?

CHAPTER TWO
EARLY AUDITIONS

Like many celebrities, the Bugatti Veyron endured a very long and at times arduous story that predated its status as an 'overnight sensation'. Rewind to 1998 and you can begin to see the genesis of the car. The Volkswagen Group announced in that year that it had acquired the Bugatti brand, previously dormant since the 1950s but for one ill-fated revival earlier in the decade. Also around this time Volkswagen had acquired a number of other prestige brands such as Bentley and Lamborghini, and had certain rights to Rolls-Royce, including the factory in Crewe, so many observers wondered why they were now taking over another elite marque. Particularly one that had been redundant for so long.

Nonetheless, the take-over was completed and the Bugatti marque was now owned by one of the most powerful and wealthy car manufacturers in the world. This in itself ruffled feathers among automotive purists, who feared that this arranged marriage between an automotive monolith and a brand renowned for its artistic flair and creativity was surely doomed to failure.

Undeterred, VW announced the esteemed Dr Karl-Heinz Neumann as Bugatti's new president. Dr Neumann was a long-term engineer at VW and was widely considered to be one of the most gifted engine experts of his generation – indeed, internally within the VW group he was known as 'The Engine Pope'. He had a reputation for not being pushed into a quicker, but inferior solution; he was a humorous, charming, laid-back person, but also honest, direct and outspoken. Because of his size and inner calm, he was also known within Volkswagen by the nickname Yogi, derived from Yogi bear. His appointment was a substantial feather in Bugatti's cap.

The brand also revealed that they had purchased the derelict Château St Jean in Molsheim, north-east France, which Ettore Bugatti – the brand's founder and namesake – had originally used as a guesthouse. Unable to prise the nearby original factory from aerospace firm Snecma, Bugatti instead announced they intended to build their own state-of-the-art assembly facility next to the château, to be called their Atelier, or 'Artist's Workshop'.

This was all very exciting and impressively confident, but what the watching world really wanted to know about was Bugatti's plans for *cars*. In 1998 the first of four concept vehicles was announced at the key French motor show, the Paris

Auto Salon. These had been designed by Giorgetto Giugiaro and his son Fabrizio of Italdesign, a prestigious design firm based in Montcalieri, near Turin. Giugiaro Senior was a renowned Italian car designer with an enviable portfolio of supercars to his name, such as the Ferrari 250 Berlinetta Bertone, the Maserati Bora and Lamborghini Cala. In 1999 he'd been named Car Designer of the Century, so his appointment was a clear statement of intent from the new executives behind Bugatti. As with many celebrities, you will often find very powerful and revered industry insiders behind the scenes.

The three cars Giugiaro oversaw were the Bugatti EB118, the EB218 and the so-called EB 18/3 Chiron. The first concept car, the EB118, was a two-door coupe with 555bhp, produced by a 6.3-litre turbocharged W18 engine (a first for a passenger car) using permanent all-wheel drive. Perhaps most striking was the presence of two front axles! This was to accommodate the proposed – and controversial – all-wheel steering. Giugiaro's curvaceous body design echoed that of the classic Bugatti Type 57 Atalante and elements of the mythical Atlantic (more of which later) too, most obviously a raised strip running along the entire centre of the car's body. Giugiaro himself said it was 'intended to be a worthy successor to the Bugatti Royale'.

When the EB118 was first shown at the Paris Motor Show in October 1998, it was effectively Bugatti's first public appearance as a revived marque, some forty years after the brand had last showcased a car in the French capital. The EB118 was destined to remain a concept and was never produced.

However, this concept was the precursor to the rather different EB218, a far grander four-door limousine/sedan which Bugatti unveiled at the Geneva Auto Salon in 1999. Bugatti purists looked to the marque's similarly long-wheelbased 1926 Royale for a precedent, although the latter's style was far more striking. As with the EB118, there were other finer 'Bugatti' aesthetics, such as elegant teardrop windows and an exquisitely initialled EB petrol cap, which signified the historic eye for detail. This concept vehicle was particularly true to Giugiaro Senior's design ethos for the brand, as he was quoted as saying, 'In my opinion, a Bugatti should be a large saloon car with a front engine.'

A few months later, at the International Automobile Exhibition in Frankfurt, the brand then introduced the Bugatti 18/3 Chiron, named after the greatest Bugatti racing driver of the inter-war era (and also the oldest man to ever compete in a grand prix, aged fifty-eight). The Chiron concept car is notable for being forged by a design team supplemented by one Hartmut Warkuss, working alongside Italdesign's Fabrizio Giugiaro. The same W18 engine was transplanted into this new car, whose chassis was itself based in part on the viciously fast Lamborghini Diablo VT, but presented here with typical Bugatti flair. This time it was a mid-engined layout and was unashamedly a supercar.

The EB118's W18 engine was later used on its successor, the EB218. The power-to-weight ratio was tremendous, helped by the fact the car's body was made using aluminium space-frame technology.

BUGATTI VEYRON – A QUEST FOR PERFECTION

With the benefit of hindsight, the EB118's nose has a definite similarity to the eventual Veyron design, albeit somewhat more pinched and slight.

On superficial inspection, the Chiron's curved nose has very clear stylistic similarity to the eventual Veyron. Made from carbon fibre, the car was extremely lightweight and was presented in a striking blue: 'Blu Côte d'Azur'. There was a retractable rear wing too, used here to improve aerodynamics with three variable settings. Notably, the engine was not fully covered and other design details such as the radiator, inset front lights and circular rear windows would also make the final cut of the Veyron. The historical nods to the brand's heritage were there too, with the 20-inch eight-spoke wheels aping those originally found on the racing driver Louis Chiron's own Type 35B racer from the 1930s.

A very notable difference from the previous concept cars was the much less luxurious interior, mimicking numerous contemporary super sports cars rather than extravagant limousines. Only one Chiron was ever built; at the time there was speculation about which concept car would eventually move into production, either the Chiron or the EB218 sedan. If it was to be the Chiron, reports suggested it would retail at around $270,000.

All three cars were notably more understated than the eventual Veyron; similarly their power, although impressive, was almost half that of the Bugatti that finally went into series production; the car world watched, was neatly impressed but not altogether blown away.

In the spring of 1999 Bugatti had produced a lavish and limited-edition hardback book that featured the first two of these three concept cars, chronicling their splendour in fine detail. In the introduction to *Marque, Legend, Renaissance*, VW group chief executive Dr Ferdinand Piëch was interviewed by author Herbert Völker. Piëch's own grandfather Ferdinand Porsche was a contemporary of Bugatti's namesake and founder, Ettore, born just six years apart, and both men were destined to indelibly change the face of the fledgling car industry.

In among the interview's references to Ferdinand Porsche and the Bugatti brand, there was a sentence from Dr Piëch that in retrospect was perhaps a hidden clue as to what this seminal automotive figurehead was looking to do next: 'The season of the exceptional is upon us again.'

This genetic desire to produce 'the best' had surely been passed down to Dr Piëch from his grandfather Ferdinand Porsche, but he declined to dwell on this, saying, 'I'm fundamentally a forward-looking person.' And Piëch made no secret of the burning ambition that his new creations would be nothing less than ground breaking: 'The Bugattis that we make will earn their image by featuring advanced technology. They will be the most ultra-modern, technologically inspiring cars of our time – no more or less than that! They will play in a league in which anything is possible.' He talked about the EB118 and EB218 but hinted at something special round the corner: 'Before long we hope to have something truly

exceptional to show for our efforts – leading edge technology and outstanding design. Rest assured, we shall not prove unfaithful to Ettore Bugatti's legacy!'

So what did Piëch mean? The concept cars had excited many but, if one was being churlish, they were not necessarily ground breaking or market leading. Ultimately, these cars would not make the final cut, destined to only ever be auditionees of the star-making process.

So what did Piëch have up his sleeve?

It was at the Geneva Motor Show in 2000 that he revealed his hand . . .

CHAPTER THREE

ATTEMPTS NO.1 AND 2

My largely self-indulgent quest to drive a Bugatti Veyron – parading as 'in the public interest' – was not without its obvious challenges. Who in their right mind would let a complete stranger drive a €1 million-plus car? Especially when they found out I was not a professional, nor even a good amateur driver. As I've already said, I am not a motoring journalist, so I cannot pretend to boast of being a seasoned vehicle tester/ reviewer. The driving skills and wordsmithery of motoring journalists should never be underestimated; when you read a 'simple' 500-word review of the latest everyday BMW or Ford, never forget that there are years of expertise rammed into those deceptively complex articles.

In my defence, I'm not a total supercar virgin. I have been lucky enough to drive a number of fast cars owned by celebrity clients and friends, but nothing in the Veyron's league. A Ferrari 355, for example, but that is a veritable slowcoach by comparison. A Lotus Elise? Little more than a tortoise. So how would I actually drive a Veyron if I was lucky enough to get in one? After all, accelerating from 0 to 60 in 2.5 seconds is one thing, but one slip of the right foot and I'd be doing 100mph-plus in just over another two seconds. At which point I'd most likely prang it. Which wouldn't be pretty. A new fender to replace the one I might dent? About £7000. Conceivably, if I got it properly wrong, I could end up being a famous clip on YouTube, or worse still, I might come home in a box.

There were specific practicalities bothering me, too. How would I insure myself? Who would pay for the petrol? And where do I put my suitcase? Does it take an iPod and is there one of those spring-out coffee holders for my obligatory slosh of caffeine? These were all important questions that troubled me right from the start.

There were other questions in my mind that started to make self-doubt

my closest companion on the quest. If I did get to drive one – and that was a big 'if' – what if I didn't like the car when I got in there? By that point, I'd be many months of writing down a path that had ultimately led to disappointment. It would be like finding the Holy Grail and thinking, 'Well, it's a nice cup and all that, but what's the fuss about?'

And worst of all – the ultimate sleep-taker – was, 'What if ultimately no one will trust me to drive their pride and joy and I don't get to drive a Veyron after all? That would have rendered all my efforts largely pointless. How could I possibly write about the Veyron if I'd never even met the 'celebrity' in question?

I don't have contacts in the motor trade. I don't obviously know 'someone who knows someone'. So, my first thought was to phone up those track-day companies, Red Letter Days and the like. If they offered a morning in a Veyron, I could just book it, go over and, bingo, job done.

Or so I thought.

Perhaps not surprisingly for a car that often costs in excess of £1 million, there's currently no UK supplier of track days in a Veyron. Undeterred, I made what I felt was a cunning swerve, *Well, I'll hire one then.* So I got on the internet and phoned one such hire company up.

'Hello, I'd like to get some prices on hiring one of your cars, please.'

'Yes, of course, sir, which car are you thinking of hiring?'

'The Bugatti Veyron.'

Slight pause.

'OK, well, that's obviously a high-end prestige car and it comes in at a base price of £17,500 for a day with a mileage limit of 100 miles per day.'

'Right . . .'

Endearingly misreading the disappointment in my voice, the very helpful lady said, 'Or we can arrange a weekend hire for £45,000, or a week is in the region of £122,000 . . .'

'Er, I don't think that will be necessary . . . thanks for your help, bye.'

I didn't ask what the deposit would have been.

CHAPTER FOUR

A TROUBLED GENESIS

Following on from the EB118, the EB218 and the Chiron, the next concept car from Bugatti was the EB 18/4 Veyron, first shown at the Tokyo Motor Show in 1999. This concept was designed by Hartmut Warkuss with Volkswagen's own designer Jozef Kaban having styled the exterior. It shared the same Diablo chassis as the Chiron and also the W18 engine, but from a styling point of view, the car was now looking very similar to the eventual production Veyron. However, there would later prove to be major problems melding the very wide 18-cylinder engine used on the previous Bugatti concept cars to this new model, so shortly afterwards the decision was taken to instead use a smaller W16 engine – hence the eventual production car's name, the Veyron 16.4 (16 cylinders, 4 turbos).

With the Veyron concept soon being upgraded to 'advanced concept' status, the car world watched in anticipation as the reality of such a mesmerising vehicle approached. However, it was at the Geneva Motor Show in March 2000 that fantasy appeared to be about to become reality, when VW group chairman Dr Piëch made the announcement that the whole motoring world had been waiting to hear: Bugatti was going to produce a car with 1001bhp; 'This will be the most exciting and most advanced car of its time, no more, no less.' Behind the scenes it was widely known that Piëch had demanded four characteristics for this new car: a 0–60mph time of less than three seconds; a top speed of 250mph; 1001bhp in the engine; and finally, most bizarrely, he required the car to be so easy to use that 'you can drive it to the opera'. If achieved, this combination of world record-shattering performance and everyday ease of use would be truly unprecedented.

Whispers of the Veyron's potential performance capabilities began to be confirmed by the striking stats coming out of VW HQ, so interest in the car was greater than ever. Behind the scenes, Bugatti engineers were by now scouring the globe for the finest exponents and manufacturers of each part, intent on only populating their supply chain with the absolute finest elements, by means of strenuous testing and quality control, including multiple factory visits and detailed local inspections. Then, in late 2001, Bugatti announced they had made the decision to commence serial production of the Veyron, with the first cars scheduled to roll out of the new assembly facility in Molsheim in 2003.

A variant of the eventual W16 engine in the Veyron had previously been seen in a similar form on the 1999 Bentley Hunaudières concept, complete with four turbochargers.

Publicly, Bugatti paraded the Veyron concept car around numerous high-profile car shows and events around the world to tease the public and enlist potential customers. It was vital that while the engineering brains wrestled with some of the most complex and demanding challenges ever faced by a team building a road-going car (at this point it was still press released as an 'experimental car'), the brand itself needed to maintain public interest in their project. So between 2002 and the car's eventual launch, the Veyron was exhibited at various supercar shows and other prestigious events around the world. For example, the first appearance of the Veyron show car in America came in August 2002 at the 17th Concorso Italiano, an annual supercar exhibition which litters the Quail Lodge Country and Golf Club in Carmel Valley, California, with a glittering array of some of the world's most desirable cars. Road-going supercars line up alongside pure-bred race cars, all of which are salivated over by the numerous VIPs and many thousands among the general public who attend the show. This was an ideal event to introduce America to the new famous face of supercar technology. In their own press release for the event, Bugatti themselves used the following phrase: 'The car was one of the most remarkable *celebrities* at the presentation of exceptional sports cars' (my italics). At most of these events, the arrival of the Veyron was the first time the car had been seen in that country, so the subsequent publicity and interest was huge.

Bugatti always seemed at pains to display their heritage and the Veyron

would invariably be displayed alongside numerous vintage masterpieces from their illustrious past. The choice of events was not casual either: many of these yachting tournaments, thoroughbred racehorse meetings and supercar exhibitions were, of course, populated by the successful and ultra-wealthy, all potential customers for the eventual car but also highly regarded opinion-formers in the sort of circles where spending a million pounds on a vehicle is not unusual. At some shows a full-scale mock-up was available, offering the potential customer the opportunity to try out the car's seating position. Bugatti mined this market heavily and by their own later admission (in 2003) 'there [was] hardly a metropolitan area that hasn't seen the advanced model'.

Back at base, superficially the feverish development was also going well. As early as the end of July 2002 Bugatti were reporting that the 16-cylinder engine had 'successfully absolved the trial runs on the testing stand' over a period of several weeks. It was during this testing spell that the innovative drive train first delivered the mythical 1000+bhp (736kW), with a corresponding torque of 1250Nm. Following the successful engine trials on the testing stand, the car was able to move outside and on to the road for more detailed examination. So in early August 2002, on the test grounds of VW's Ehra-Lessien test track near Wolfsburg, the Veyron 16.4 first emerged into the morning sun. The aim of this phase was to fine-tune the engine specifically but also to generally test the car as a whole. Everything was going brilliantly . . . or was it?

The 16.4 concept car; there was also a 1999 concept car submitted by the then-SEAT head of design, Walter de'Silva, to Hartmut Warkuss. A full-scale mock-up was even built and presented, but ultimately rejected.

By 2003 Bugatti was confidently suggesting the Veyron would soon commence manufacture. Indeed, at the 73rd Geneva Motor Show that spring, they preceded their announcement of the car's appearance by saying that 'as per current planning' this was to be the last appearance of the 'show car', ahead of a commercial release later that year. After Geneva the plan was to enter the so-called 'hot phase' of development, immediately prior to the actual production and delivery of the very first models. As a precursor to this, the 'genuine' Veyron – as against the less complete 'show car' – was scheduled to be shown at the Art de l'Automobile in Monte Carlo.

However, in July of that year, the project suffered a major and very embarrassing hiccup. Taking to the Laguna Seca race track in California for a classic Bugatti event, the car spun into a gravel pit on the very first lap, only narrowly missing a concrete wall. It was a very public humiliation but also, more worryingly, the tip of an iceberg.

For many journalists this was a very public demonstration of the rumoured problems that the ambitious project was suffering. The chief concern among these writers seemed to be how on earth to cool that colossal engine. Problems with this issue were cited as the key reason for potential delays while others speculated there were multiple debilitating obstacles such as the gearbox, tyres and electronic difficulties.

Bugatti president Dr Karl-Heinz Neumann tackled the cooling accusation head on and cited successful tests run at an external temperature of 40°C, which verified the Veyron engine running at its top speed unaffected. Other rumours suggested that due to these possibly insurmountable issues the eventual street version of the car would actually be a diluted vehicle with less power and a reduced performance, again denied: 'There isn't the slightest reason why limits should be set with the vehicle's top speed – there will be no other version of this vehicle!' Bugatti was challenged on multiple occasions about the likelihood of the April 2004 launch date being met but the company denied repeatedly and unequivocally that there would be any delay.

Yet still the doubts persisted. The VW group was also in the midst of cost-cutting measures which further fuelled the sceptics' increasingly barbed jibes. This stringent economy drive compared to the cost of the Veyron did not go unnoticed. When questioned by probing journalists about the sense of injecting a rumoured £1.5 billion into the Bugatti project, VW were keen to stress this represented no more than 40 per cent of what BMW sinks into Formula 1. Unconvinced, some sceptics even christened the troubled era 'Piëch's folly'.

Journalistic fingers were pointed at board level too: the omnipotent Dr Piëch retired as chairman of the VW group and had handed over to Bernd Pischetsrieder in April 2002. When the new head of the VW group was interviewed by German

magazine *Stern* he was asked, 'Are you really thinking of launching the Veyron in the course of 2004? It has become a little quiet around this car.' Pischetsrieder countered with great confidence: 'On the contrary, it has become relatively noisy. At present, the usual tests and trials are being run, and some of these vehicles produce a rather heavy engine noise . . . in April of 2004 we shall deliver the first one.'

The press scepticism did not let up, however, reinforced by the postponement of a planned media test premiere which was blamed on the steering system not yet being perfect. In early September the VW chairman was further moved to refute rumours reported in the *Frankfurter Allgemeine Sonntagszeitung* that the project was indeed falling behind. After pointing out that the car was widely considered to be the most advanced and challenging development project of the modern automotive era, Pischetsrieder said that he was satisfied with the engine performance results on the test bed and stated there were no problems with the vehicle's engine or transmission, despite reports to the contrary. Pischetsrieder rounded off by saying the project was in its closing stages of development and that the first cars would still be delivered to customers in April 2004.

With more reports surfacing and whispering about further delays, Bugatti were forced to react yet again shortly after. This time the brand's own president, Dr Karl-Heinz Neumann, spoke to the press to clarify that the project was

In the intervening development years, the exact colour and trim specs changed multiple times, but that was insignificant compared to the feverish development going on under the bonnet and indeed all over the internal workings of the car. In fact, at first the publicly displayed 'show' models were barely capable of driving at all; the real 1000+bhp monsters were being kept under closely guarded wraps by the elite team of engineers in Wolfsburg.

'running according to plan'. Having overseen the project from the beginning, it was difficult for Dr Neumann to hide his discontent at the media snipers, gossip which he referred to as 'miserably researched reports in the media', which he said had left him 'not amused'. 'According to everything I've read about the vehicle up to now, what we should be presenting here today is nothing more than a pile of junk.'

Unimpressed, media snipers suggested this might prove to be the automotive world's biggest and most costly white elephant ever. Was it really on the brink? In an article in the *Sunday Times*, writer Andrew Frankel asked, 'Has VW bitten off more than it can chew?' For a brand whose founder Ettore Bugatti prided himself on his prototypes almost always being produced, the tension was almost unbearable.

Further changes within the hierarchy of Bugatti with incoming and outgoing presidents of the project only served to fuel the rumours that the car was in trouble. Dr Neumann had retired in late 2003, having been at VW for thirty-eight years. The new Bugatti president, Dr Thomas Bscher, was a very canny appointment by the brand. The former private banker (born into the Pferdmenges family who partly owned the esteemed German private bank Sal. Oppenheim) was also a LeMans racer himself; he was not only chosen because of his obvious automotive expertise but also because of his knowledge of future Bugatti clientele. This was an area in which the VW group had no previous experience at such an ultra-wealthy level. Bscher took over the complex project and these very senior retirements and new executive blood quickly prompted a chain of events that eventually led to a shocking announcement.

Before he went, Dr Neumann had reiterated the planned production cycle, saying that the completion of the factory meant they were able to commence the manufacture of the first pre-series car by the end of the year, with commercial production still set for April 2004. 'Nothing now stands in the way of production.' Internal reasons were cited by some sources as the continued reliance on this date, but seasoned observers knew that even with Dr Neumann's extensive expertise and engine genius, what Bugatti were trying to create was a first. The situation was perhaps best described by the revered automotive journalist Eddie Alterman in an article he wrote for *GQ*: 'Every solution for achieving the 1001 bhp cascaded into a new problem: Can the gearbox take the power? No, it must be strengthened. Can the driveline take a stronger gearbox? No, it needs all-wheel drive. Can the brakes cope? No, the car needs bigger ones, which means bigger wheels. Can the suspension handle bigger wheels? No, it needs bigger wishbones. And so on. Thus think of the Veyron not as the world's fastest automobile but as the greatest number of engineering challenges ever overcome by one vehicle.'

With this undeniable backdrop of seemingly insurmountable challenges, in March 2004 – just a month before the original planned delivery of vehicles to customers – Dr Neumann's successor in the top role, Dr Bscher, made an announcement at the Geneva Motor Show that shocked the car world (although many had indeed predicted this development): the Veyron would be delayed after all. Dr Bscher's candid words were very honest: 'Picture a diamond, which must be carefully cut and polished before the breadth of its brilliance can be revealed. Following in the footsteps of Ettore Bugatti, the Veyron too will be brought to technical perfection. This takes time. And we will take the time we need.' It later transpired that along with Bscher, the VW chairman Bernd Pischetsrieder had also been a very vocal advocate of delaying the project after all, *to get it right*.

How long, exactly? The Bugatti announcement offered this: 'Somewhat more time than originally anticipated is needed both to meet these unusually high standards, which Bugatti Automobiles itself has set the Veyron in every aspect imaginable, as well as to provide the customer the perfection he has every right to expect from such a unique vehicle. The first vehicles for this exclusive clientele will thus be delivered in the second half of 2005.' So it was a delay of more than a year.

Dr Bscher himself had been unhappy with the car when he took over as Bugatti president and he was instrumental in taking the decision to delay the launch. Bugatti then brought in the revered mechanical engineer Dr Franz-Josef Paefgen as CEO of Bugatti Engineering and he subsequently recruited Dr Wolfgang Schreiber as chief engineer for the Veyron. Schreiber was the mastermind behind VW's revolutionary DSG gearbox and was widely seen as one of the most talented and elite of a new generation of automotive engineers. However, the question still remained: would the Veyron ever see the light of day?

In that year's delay, the car's development was extensively reviewed. A crack team was assembled by Dr Schreiber working from the secret research and development workshop in Wolfsburg, Germany, home to the VW group's HQ. The eyes of the car world were on Schreiber and his team. In Wolfsburg there were about ninety people, most of whom were in-house Volkswagen employees (as opposed to external aerospace experts, as the urban myth suggests). There was, of course, some support from external companies in certain areas of development and a handful of experts were also brought in from race-car companies.

With suitable panache, the first official Bugatti press releases of 2005 neatly airbrushed the delay into relative insignificance, such that by late January of that year the company was excited to announce that 'Development of the Bugatti EB 16.4 Veyron is on track and progressing well.' The newly focused team made rapid progress and by the autumn of 2005 they were ready to reveal their work to the waiting press hordes at the aforementioned media launch in Sicily.

The Bugatti Veyron 16.4 was *finally* ready to go into full series production.

CHAPTER FIVE
ATTEMPT NO.3

I've already said that I don't know 'people' within the motor industry. With my Red Letter Day and rental plans in tatters, I decided to work with what I do know: people in the entertainment and music business. I had worked with several celebrities and musicians who were avid car collectors and had even enjoyed various bouts of motorway madness as a passenger in a number of supercars. I had a feeling one particular musical bête noir would fancy himself in a Veyron. So I made some phone calls only to find he had just recently parted ways with his management company; more phone calls were made and eventually I got through to his brand-new manager, who, it turned out, had only been working with him a few days. He listened politely as I explained my quest.

'I'm not exactly sure what's in his garage at the moment, to be perfectly honest, but I'm seeing him tomorrow, so I'll ask for sure . . .'

Great. I was in with a chance.

The next day came and went, as did the one after that. I was starting

to get the sweats at night. This could be my last chance, the clutching of automotive straws. Then, four days later, my mobile rang.

I pounced on my phone. This was it, I could almost feel my lily white ass sitting in that sumptuous Veyron's leather seat.

'Hi, Martin, yes, I've spoke to [famous person] about his car . . .'

'Yes . . . ?'

'You were right about him owning a Veyron . . .'

'Fantast—'

'But . . .'

'But what . . . ?'

'He's sold it.'

Crap.

I was gutted, this had been my A1 route, my dead cert. Gone. How selfish of him to sell it without even checking with me first. It was beginning to feel like trying to catch water.

CHAPTER SIX

A BRIEF HISTORY OF SUPERCARS

So Bugatti had finally managed to get this remarkable car launched and into production. But what exactly was the context for their brave/foolhardy project? Where were supercars 'at' when the Veyron was launched?

It's worth taking our foot off the metaphorical accelerator for a moment to detail the automotive genre within which the Veyron sits – supercars. The history of this glittering motoring subculture is well documented, yet it's appropriate to revisit briefly the chronology here because there are common threads in the numerous headline acts we find scattered throughout its long-running bill.

The modern use of the term is widely attributed to L. J. K. Setright, an English-born motoring journalist of Australian descent. He was a qualified lawyer but turned his back on the courts as he disliked practising law so intensely (he also spent time as an RAF air-traffic controller while fulfilling his National Service). However, it was as a long-standing writer for CAR magazine across three decades that 'LJKS' made his mark. His writing style was – like the supercars he christened – extravagant, unusual, ornate. In his obituary in 2005, the Daily Telegraph described him as, 'Britain's best-known and most eloquent motoring journalist, famous in an era before car experts could win easy notoriety on TV.' His interest in engineering innovation was probably inherited: his father was the inventor of the eponymous Setright ticket machine, used for decades on buses and trams around the world.

But how did he come to use the term 'supercar'? In the modern era there is a general consensus on what is regarded as the first supercar: the Lamborghini Miura. This is the car of which LJKS himself used the phrase in a 1966 piece published by CAR. Others claim it was already in use in America for affordable mid-sized V8s which took their genetics from the drag strip; elsewhere specific writers have championed the memorable Ford GT40 road-legal models as early 'supercars'. Many Italian purists hold up the beautiful 250 GTO as the Prancing Horse's early contender. The 1960 Rambler Rebel was described as such and is widely quoted as another early example, alongside 'street racers' like the Pontiac GTO. Indeed, the 'SC' in SC Rambler was said to stand for 'Supercar'. Yet half a decade before the Rambler, Mercedes had introduced the first fuel-injected road car, the audacious gull-winged 300SL. Surely that was a supercar?

Some sources reference a metal shortage around the Second World War as pushing car manufacturers to develop lighter – and therefore faster – cars, so there are many historical reference points in the genealogy of the supercar. Other sources go back much, much earlier, citing an advertisement in the 11 November 1920 edition of *The Times* for a high-performance car called the Ensign Six which said, 'If you are interested in a supercar, you cannot afford to ignore the claims of the Ensign 6.' So although there is some argument over who actually coined the term, and indeed what was the very first of the breed, what there is no doubting is that supercars themselves have fascinated millions of car lovers for decades.

The Lamborghini Miura is a neat starting point for many because its manufacturer seems to sum up what a supercar is all about. As a child, I had a poster of a Lamborghini Countach on my wall, still considered by many to be the most bonkers – and therefore, in spirit, the greatest – supercar of all time, christened by some as the 'King of Supercars'. For a long period Lambos were always the most visually arresting of the breed, virtually impossible to drive, yes, but at least they looked the part. Post-millennial supercars often marry aerospace technology and automotive engineering but with the Countach much of the appeal was that it actually *looked like a spaceship*. At least it did to me, a kid driving around Dudley in the back of a chocolate-brown Hillman Hunter with plastic 'leather' seats ('expanded vinyl' if you were really posh) and an engine just about big enough to open a bottle of pop.

The Countach came from supercar stock. It was with the previous decade's Miura that Lamborghini created a car that was *flamboyant*, which with its low nose and fat, powerful rear end was the poster star that spawned a generation of similar-looking vehicles. It wasn't just eye candy either – the Miura was the first production car to feature a mid-mounted engine too, which contributed in part to its appearance being so strikingly different.

The first modern supercar?
The Lamborghini Miura.

For many, the Ferrari F40 is the quintessential supercar.

The history of supercars since the 1960s has been chequered, with the oil crisis of the next decade threatening to extinguish the subculture altogether. Yet even in these dark days, the appeal of a car that is worth so much money and performs like a race car for the road endured: 1974 saw the Ferrari 365BB and the Countach, a year later the Porsche 911 Turbo ruffled many feathers with its rear-engined brutality and extravagant spoilers. The decade of excess saw the 1980s filled with many extravagant cars; when Group B racing demanded 200 road-going versions of the racers in order to be eligible to compete, motoring madness returned to the roads with stunning cars such as Ferrari's 288GTO (the first super sports car to top 300km/h), which was followed by unrelated statements such as the Porsche 959, that itself boasted a blistering time of just over four seconds for the 0–60 sprint.

Ferrari responded with the bonkers F40, stripped out and brutally fast, a car which most eight-year-old boys end up drawing when you ask them to sketch their own 'supercar' (it was the first road-legal car to break 200mph). Then when the Diablo replaced Lambo's Countach, supercar fans breathed a sigh of relief that the genre was still alive and lunatic.

The blisteringly quick Porsche 959.

As cynics were no doubt warning Bugatti during the development of the Veyron, there have always been polarised fortunes in this high-cost, high-risk sector. The demise of the lamented Jaguar XJ220 came in the same year as Bugatti's short-lived relaunch with the EB110 (more of which later), at the time the fastest car in the world at 218mph.

Then along came the Big Daddy of modern supercars . . . the McLaren F1. So ahead of its time and so far in front of the competition was this masterpiece that for well over a decade all other 'supercars' would be compared negatively to this landmark creation. In all those years, nothing – not the Ferrari F50 'F1 car for the road', 911 GT2s, the Pagani Zonda etc. – would come close to the McLaren F1. Until 2005 . . .

For some time, the phrase 'hypercars' had been used to describe the very best of the best, the cars that inhabit a rarefied elite of vehicles whose performance – and usually cost – sets them apart from even the more 'regular' supercars. But even that new word wasn't enough, it seemed. The website Motorsportcircuitguide.com even attributes the demise of the word 'supercar' to the great McLaren F1, which it said effectively forced the invention of the phrase 'ultimate supercar' just to accommodate its brilliance; thus supercar became hypercar and now we have 'ultracar'. For me, I think 'supercar' suffices, not as a nostalgic nod to lost writing heroes like LJKS but just because it does the job. Otherwise, where we do end? Super-dupercars? Ultra-mega-cars? . . .

I digress. Regardless of what you choose to call them, supercars have long been a staple of the motor-loving world, a sparkling sign of engineering innovation, automotive ambition and personal success. This is the world into which the Bugatti Veyron was born . . . and into which I was trying to land.

The majestic McLaren F1. A legendary moment in supercar history.

CHAPTER SEVEN

ATTEMPTS NO.4 AND 5
. . . (Knocking on the Front Door)

I don't know why I didn't think of this straight away: a simple test drive. You can walk into any dealership in the country and ask to try any car. That's what the glass temples of automotive seduction are there for, right? On many occasions I've swanned into, say, a Ford dealership and minutes later a mighty Escort or on one occasion a glittering Focus was all mine on the open road. Even a Lexus once, when I had an Alan Partridge moment after someone told me they were 'affordable luxury'. So why not a Veyron?

Although I suspected I'd been over-thinking my quest, I wasn't foolish enough to assume it would be quite so simple, I knew I had research to do. So I scoured the pages of *Top Marques*, the *Sunday Times* and the like for clues to the best dealerships. When I had targeted three suitable cars – there are only ever a handful of Veyrons for sale in the UK at any given moment – I decided to educate myself on the process first.

What exactly does the buyer of a Bugatti Veyron sound like when he calls a dealership? How should I behave? I called a dealer who had sold numerous former celebrity clients of mine various supercars and explained I needed his help. He didn't sell Bugattis but he was happy to give me some pointers.

'First of all, there's a high chance that the dealer will already know the prospective buyer. Because if they are genuine they've probably got a Ferrari, Lambos, Rolls; they will be into their cars.'

And if you don't know them, presumably you have to be a little bit more cautious?

'We would just get into a conversation about cars. I'd ask them what cars they've owned in the past, what they currently have in their garage, what cars they'd like to get hold of. If they know what they are talking about, you can tell. If they are after a Bugatti, they will most likely already have an Enzo or a Carrera GT, an SLR, and maybe a Range Rover that they use day to day. They might live in London but also have a Monaco address or a house in New York or the Caribbean. Someone can't really bluff talking about these sort of cars and the lifestyle that surrounds them. So their knowledge and everyday life will show through. Oh, and one more thing, genuine buyers of cars like that never ask for a test drive . . . the dealer will always offer first . . .'

So I was now ready to phone up and try to test drive a Veyron. I knew how to answer all the questions and I certainly wasn't going to ask for the test drive, but one niggling problem sat in the back of my mind. I couldn't lie, I couldn't openly tell a totally fabricated fiction; it was already a slightly uncomfortable possibility to test drive a car that I would need to win the Lottery to buy. To assuage my guilt, I bought sixteen lottery tickets that weekend, one each for the number of cylinders in the Veyron. Did I feel lucky? No, but I felt less guilty because by the time I might get the test drive, it wasn't impossible that I could buy that car.

Then I called the three dealerships that were advertising pre-owned Veyrons (notice in this rarefied supercar market they are not called 'second-hand', but 'pre-owned'). All three salesmen were on voicemail, presumably out testing some fabulous Lambo with a rich Middle Eastern prince. I left a message on each, shamelessly trying to throw my Black Country accent and sound vaguely posh (rather than drunk and/or Irish, which is what I actually sounded like). Two never phoned me back. The third salesman did, and spoke in an impossibly posh accent.

He asked me what car I was looking at.

'A Bugatti Veyron.'

Slight pause.

As predicted, he then asked me a little bit about my own car history. 'You are clearly a car fanatic to be looking at the Bugatti, Mr Roach. Presumably you have a long history of buying supercars. Out of interest, what was your first?'

I just couldn't do it. I couldn't lie.

'It was a Morris Marina estate, bottle green.'

'OK, I see Mr Roach, well, listen, my next customer's literally just walked in, can I call you back later . . . ?'

He didn't call back.

I was relieved. I'd been dreading telling him about my Ford Escort Acapulco.

Oh, and in case you wondered, the sixteen Lottery tickets drew a blank too.

My phone book had run dry. My 'brainwaves' had all been fruitless. I'd spent months on the phone, emailing people, scratching my head, but I was getting nowhere. With my book's deadline looming large, I was staring at a humiliating failure. I'd fallen spectacularly short in trying to climb this impossible mountain. It was no use, like Frodo and Sam sitting exhausted at the gates of Mordor, I had no other option. I had to go and knock on the front door. I needed to contact Bugatti.

I had deliberately not approached Bugatti directly as this was never going to be an official book, I had no intention of offering them approval of the text and also why would they help someone from outside their inner circle, and over whom they had no control? Besides, the only link I had with the brand was the 'Contact' form on their website. Me and a million other web browsers.

You may have been thinking if I've ghosted David Coulthard, surely he could have phoned them up and secured me a drive? My celebrity ace card, so to speak. He's certainly one of the funniest and most charming ghost clients I've ever worked with and has in the past been at pains (despite the not inconsiderable inconvenience) to help me. The phone call to him was – as ever – highly entertaining but sadly 'DC' had never worked with Bugatti directly.

The problem was, I only had two contacts in the world of automobiles and Coulthard was one of them. So that was the first of my two automotive bolts shot. Still not convinced, I hear you say. Surely my phone book is filled with 'E' for Ecclestone and 'D' for Dennis. Not so. My feet are sticky with the excesses of celebrity, remember, not the oil of the pits. Coulthard was precisely 50 per cent of my contacts in the motoring world; the 'other half' so to speak was a man who appears to possess one of the human race's largest brains. I had previously worked as editor with an esteemed neuroscientist, Dr Kerry Spackman, on his best-selling book *The Winner's Bible*. Dr Spackman was predominantly a neuroscientist and award-winning mathematician, but his unique combination of skills had increasingly seen him a sought-after mentor in the arena of elite sports performance, having worked alongside Sir Jackie Stewart for McLaren F1, Jaguar's racing team, as well as the All Blacks and numerous Olympians.

He was literally my last chance. However, what worried me as I looked at the last bullet in my metaphorical gun was that I recalled Dr Spackman once saying that motor racing and the motor industry were often two separate universes. However, I was now so desperate that he was the equivalent of Obi-Wan Kenobi, my only hope. Maybe, just maybe, he knew someone at Bugatti.

I phoned him up in New Zealand.

'Morning, evening, Kerry . . .'

We exchanged pleasantries and he told me about the work he'd been doing with the Kiwi Olympic team (I wonder if any of those drive a . . .) and then I just came right out and asked him.

'Kerry, do you know anyone at Bugatti?'

'I don't, no. Sorry . . .'

Foiled again.

'But I used to teach Dr Ulrich Eichhorn, 'he was the Director of Research at Volkswagen and then moved to Bentley.'

'He's the what-of-the-what-what? Did I hear you correctly?'

He repeated his connection and said he was happy to give Dr Eichhorn a call then ring me back with any news. Okay, it wasn't Bugatti, but Dr Eichhorn would represent my first and only chink of light into the VW group.

I put the phone down and sat staring blankly out of the window. I was back in the game.

Or was I? A few anxious days passed but the phone didn't ring. I knew from working with Dr Spackman that he was meticulous, so if he had any news he would have rung back straightaway. As I sat and waited, I knew the lack of a call could only mean one thing: yet another dead-end. An overwhelming sense of gloom washed over me.

My mood lightened slightly when Dr Spackman called back four days later and said he'd tracked down Dr Eichorn and was hoping to talk to him that night. I knew that Dr Spackman was working very long hours with a number of Olympians and that helping me on my quest would necessarily have to take a back-seat. The problem was, I just didn't have the time but it's difficult to phone someone up and say, 'Would you mind terribly if that Olympic champion just holds the line, while you sort me out a jolly in the Bugatti?'

So I left Dr Spackman well alone. Two weeks passed and I began to think this quest was over after all. One Sunday morning at 7 a.m., after having pored over my phone book one last time to no avail and having pressed 'Get Mail' for what seemed like a thousand times (nothing from Dr Spackman), I finally gave up. I was at a loss. First thing Monday morning I'd have to call the publisher and come clean, the drive just wasn't going to happen. Even for Dr Spackman, who seems to not understand the word 'impossible', it was an ask too far. I switched off my Mac and went for a run.

An hour later after pounding the hills while trying desperately to collate my thoughts about what I could possibly do next to fulfil my quest now that Obi-Wan had drawn a blank, I came back indoors, tired, dejected and out of options.

The message light was flashing on my answerphone. It was a warm Kiwi accent.

'Hey, Martin, it's Kerry here. You are going to Bugatti and you are going to drive a Veyron!'

CHAPTER EIGHT

AN AFTERNOON WITH THE DOCTOR

Within two weeks of that phone call I was sitting on a plane heading to Wolfsburg, Germany, where the Bugatti Veyron was masterminded at a deceptively modest research facility. A combination of sheer luck (Dr Spackman knowing Dr Eichhorn), my book's premise (that the car was a bona-fide celebrity and was therefore next on my list of superstars to work with) plus my own portfolio had, it turned out, intrigued Bugatti. As I've mentioned, I hadn't initially previously approached them because I knew that they had politely turned down several approaches to write books about the brand and even specific ones about the Veyron itself. But my quest to meet their celebrity had, it seemed, tickled their fancy. They had read my proposal, spoken to a few celebrity references and, to my delight, offered to show me the Veyron in person. The email confirming this exciting news used the words 'test drive', which I assumed would mean my own opportunity to drive the actual car. Wouldn't it?

On arrival at Hanover airport, a pristine VW people-carrier picked me up and glided me to VW's nearby HQ, the so-called Autostadt (or 'Car City'), a Willy Wonka-style showpiece 'village' sitting in twenty-five hectares next to the VW manufacturing plant in Wolfsburg. As we pulled up alongside this huge theme park, four towering red-brick chimneys framed the far side of the site, instantly reminding me of Battersea Power Station. Held aloft next to one of the towers and overlooking Wolfsburg itself is a gigantic circular VW logo, looking very much like the world's biggest pin badge. The redevelopment of this former car park began in 1994 and nearly £400 million later it had been transformed into a thriving community of tourists and workers. The Autostadt includes a customer centre, factory tour, test track, cinema and various exhibits showcasing Volkswagen's history. Each year over two million visitors pass through its doors; since its grand opening in 2000, it has become one of Germany's key tourist attractions with seventeen million visitors to date.

After being dropped off, I stepped out into a freezing cold winter wind, the temperature was −5°C and the previous weekend's snowfall was still piled up at the side of the road. As I walked across to the main hall, I noticed a landscaped infinity pool which was frozen solid, its surface scattered with fallen pine cones

The 'Type 57' variant of the Bugatti Atlantic is now arguably the most expensive car of all time. Bugatti only ever built four; one recently sold privately to an unknown American collector for $35 million.

sticking half out of the thick ice covering. Not ideal conditions for testing the world's fastest ever road car. My mind was cast back to the launch of the Veyron in Russia, a particularly hair-raising day for the potential customers – and Bugatti no doubt! – because it was snowing.

I was met at the front desk of the Autostadt by an elegantly dressed man called Paul. He spoke perfect English, but his accent was an amalgam of regions, at first Geordie, then a dash of Swiss, some Austrian and only an occasional Scottish burr. He was my guide for the afternoon, a gesture by Bugatti to welcome me to Germany. Paul's knowledge of the site was immense, perhaps to be expected in terms of VW, but his knowledge of car history in general was equally massive. We strolled around the building and he showed me the various exhibitions and displays. There was a new section which showcased VW's commitment to sustainability, with exhibits about recycling, emissions and so on. 'Not an exhibit that we will see the Veyron in any time soon?' I asked Paul cheekily.

Most impressive of all the exhibits was a huge collection showing the history of the motor car. This includes the one-millionth Mini (bought at auction from under the nose of BMW), Doc Brown's time-travelling DeLorean DMC-12 from *Back to the Future*, as well as many early VWs, Porsches, Mercedes and so on. Star of the show for me, however, was a replica Bugatti Atlantic in that famous startling racing blue. A huge car, the external rivets and enormous nose make it look more like a cartoon than a car. That Atlantic cost an eye-watering 140,000 French francs on its launch into a world gripped by economic crisis and about to trip into a devastating world war.

The completely mirrored Veyron on display at the Premium Clubhouse at Car City, Wolfsburg.

Behind the massive Atlantic was a Bugatti Type 15, even more cartoon-like, tiny, exaggerated, surely not actually useable? It was hard not to think of how far car manufacture had come in the intervening years, especially with regard to the supercar I was trying to drive.

The final part of my tour was in a so-called 'Premium Clubhouse' building, and mysteriously Paul would only tell me that it was 'a piece of art that I think you will like'. I walked into this modernist building then down a line of steps guarded by a noticeably tall security man in a blazer. I turned the corner and that's when I saw it . . .

. . . a totally *silver* Bugatti Veyron, sitting in a completely mirrored room, clutching its stand as if it were about to start eating the floor.

The car had been completely chromed by the artist Noah Joseph and then placed in a totally mirrored room, so that every single inch of the bodywork seemed to bounce off the walls, floor and ceiling, repeated infinitely around the space. The mirrored floor in particular offered the perfect opportunity to see the underside of the car. The 'piece' was called 'Après Vous' and was said to continue Joseph's reputation for creating 'mental spaces in which he explores aesthetic perceptions'. Apparently. For me, this was just real celebrity treatment. My anticipation of the next day's test drive went up several notches.

It was in this mirrored larger-than-life showcase that I also met Emanuela Wilm, the director of Bugatti's Media Relations. She was *impossibly* stylish and spoke perfect English. We drank cappuccino and chatted about the car and – having met many PR masterminds in my time working with celebrities – I was amazed at her genuine passion and enthusiasm. Given that she had to fly around the world most weeks meeting car journalists, attending shows, working with the Bugatti team and generally smoothing the passage of the brand across the globe, she spoke about the car with a fire in her eyes that looked as if it was her first day on the job. I got a real sense of her passion when she told me about the first time that she had driven a Veyron herself. *This*, I thought to myself, *is a Bugatti person!* She informed me that the following afternoon at 1 p.m., the Veyron's chief engineer Dr Wolfgang Schreiber would pick me up for 'a drive in a Veyron'.

The hackles on my neck stood up when she mentioned Dr Schreiber. He is, after all, the man who has been repeatedly singled out as responsible for seizing the project's immense engineering complexities and getting the Veyron back on track. When she said that, I had the same goosebumps as that day the previous summer in Mayfair when I'd first seen the Grand Sport. I was nearly there.

After my tour of the Autostadt was finished, I walked back to my hotel; I'd booked into the Wolfsburg Holiday Inn, complete with 'Polo' and 'Golf' conference rooms. I sat in the bar and watched a Champions League match, surrounded by German businessmen cheering on their home team. I was left alone in the corner as they roared a last-minute goal that secured a deserved victory. It was a good match, but I couldn't stop thinking about the next day, the Veyron, the drive. After two tankards of German beer, I tried in vain to get some sleep.

The next morning I woke up at 6 a.m. First I was due to visit the offices of Dr Paefgen, the former CEO of Bugatti Engineering and latterly the president of Bugatti who had just retired earlier that month. When I arrived in the glass lift at the top floor of the Kundencenter I was met by his PA, Frau Lange, who – you've guessed it – was also impossibly stylish and spoke perfect English. We chatted in the Bugatti president's boardroom and as we did I noticed framed pictures of numerous historical landmarks from Bugatti's past: important faces, famous cars, celebrated race victories and, scattered among the old-school idols, a few photographs of the Veyron. Frau Lange spoke about her job and the car with the same passion that I'd seen in Frau Wilm the day before, as well as in my Autostadt tour guide Paul, and with the same fire that I'd see in pretty much every Bugatti person I would meet on my quest.

After bidding farewell to Frau Lange in the president's office, the rest of the morning before my test drive seemed like an eternity. I sat in my hotel room, watching rubbish hotel TV. It was the day of the last ever Space Shuttle launch, an event which cost the USA $500 million, which seemed to make the Veyron's reputed £1.5 billion development costs over nearly six years seem like a bargain.

Then suddenly a startling and rather unnerving realisation dawned on me. Now that I was in Wolfsburg, supposedly moments away from driving the object of my quest, I began to wonder what the Veyron would actually be like to drive. As I sat alone in that hotel room, I realised that I'd been so caught up in *securing* a drive that I hadn't thought about the test itself for months. As I've said, I'm a rank amateur as far as driving skills are concerned, and after months of research I was now explicitly aware of the brutal performance of the car itself.

I tried to calm my fears about the massive power and acceleration I was about to feel. Will it be easy? Or a nightmare? Frightening, even? I reassured myself that if I did get to test the Veyron, at least the isolated test track's wide tarmac and flat spin-off areas would provide a safe haven for my limited driving ability should I cock up. I'd seen the track at Ehra-Lessien on the TV many times and it looked expansive and safe, although if you come off at 200mph+, safe is a relative term. The temperature outside had warmed up slightly and was registering around two degrees, although on the walk back from Frau Lange's Bugatti office, I had noticed the infinity pool at the Autostadt was still frozen solid with those pine cones half-protruding stubbornly from the icy water.

I went to the toilet about fifteen times that morning. Dr Schreiber was due at 1 p.m. His fabulously helpful PA had said he'd pick me up for my drive in the Veyron. What I didn't realise until later was that she actually meant 'pick me up *in* the Veyron'. At my Holiday Inn. Just think about that for a moment.

After pacing up and down in my hotel room for an hour watching (but not really listening to) yet more news reports, I went down to reception at 12.30. I didn't want to be late and I figured that thirty minutes was long enough to walk from the front desk to the front door, a journey of about ten metres. So I sat down, stomach churning, and started to wait. The time moved so slowly and as it did, I began to panic and rampant self-doubt crept into my mind once again. I re-read my emails from Bugatti and to my absolute horror I couldn't tell if they were clear about whether I would actually *drive* the car or just be driven around *in it* by Dr Schreiber. I saw the words 'your test drive', but another later email said, 'Enjoy your ride in the Veyron'. Had it all been some horrible misunderstanding? Had I made an almighty mistake? If I had, in the words of Puss In Boots in *Shrek 3*, I was 'Royally f**ked'.

At 12.55 my phone rang. The incoming number told me it was Dr Schreiber's office. My heart sank. I knew it, I knew this couldn't be possible. He'd obviously changed his mind, there'd been some misunderstanding and I wouldn't, after all, be able to go out in his car. Apologies, etc. etc., terribly sorry. Sitting in that hotel reception, I was gutted by the sight of the +49 code on my phone's screen. I pressed 'Accept'.

'Hello, Mr Roach? Just to let you know that Dr Schreiber wishes to send you sincere apologies . . .'

Oh no . . . no . . . don't . . .

'. . . but he's running a little late and will be with you at around 1.20 p.m. Is that OK?'

My heart leaped at the words and I thanked the friendly Bugatti voice on the phone and hung up. What I actually could have said was, 'If I get to go in a Veyron, I'll wait here till I'm a hundred.'

In the twenty-five minutes before Dr Schreiber was due, the time passed a little quicker but doubts about getting an actual drive (rather than a passenger ride) still lingered. Then, at 1.15 p.m., the hotel muzak kicked out Coldplay's song 'The Scientist'. Sitting there alone, wracked by nerves, I listened to every word intently, trying to distract myself from the mounting anxiety. Inevitably, perhaps, my vain efforts at distraction did the opposite, and my fuddled mind just about decided that Chris Martin, charity campaigner extraordinaire and an environmentalist's champion, was actually a secret petrolhead and had in fact written the song in honour of the Veyron. He was singing of how lovely the object of his affections is, how he wanted to know their innermost secrets, he had so many questions to ask, he even spoke of 'numbers and figures' so he clearly had the Veyron's technical data in mind when he penned the tune. But above all, there was a genuinely poignant moment which seemed to sum up what the engineer who was about to pick me up at the hotel had been forced to confront and wrestle with when developing the Veyron, a striking dilemma at the very core of this remarkable car: the paradox between science and progress versus passion and 'heart'.

That seemed to sum up the Veyron for me. I had started to write a book about a car that was a celebrity; within hours of landing in Wolfsburg, I had realised this was as much about the *people* as it was the car; and further, you could sense the one underlying, burning characteristic of everyone involved with this project, behind all the engineering, the technical data and the science: *passion*.

I didn't listen to the rest of the Coldplay song though because I then heard a distant rumble on the road. I'd mistakenly 'heard' the Veyron about fifty times in the hour I'd sat in reception, but of course every 'supercar' engine I thought I was hearing so far had actually turned out to be a lorry, a motorbike or a knackered old Peugeot. But this sound was different, and I knew this time it was something special arriving because as I looked up, a man on a bicycle nearly crashed into a bush while craning his neck to see.

I craned my own neck around the tall reception window again . . .

That's when I saw it . . .

A gleaming Bugatti Veyron, clutching the road as if it were about to start eating the tarmac.

The first words out of my mouth?

'It's orange and black. It's orange and black.'

Orange and black could only mean one thing.

It was a Super Sport.

1200bhp.

The fastest production car ever built. The world record holder.

Picking me up from a Holiday Inn.

I walked to the front door and as the Super Sport pulled on to the forecourt, Dr Schreiber flashed his lights and rolled gently towards me. For some reason, I know not why, I saluted. It just felt like a really important VIP had turned up. I was overwhelmed by excitement.

Dr Schreiber pulled up and, with the engine still running, stepped out of the Veyron and walked over to me, shaking my hand firmly with a crisp and warm smile on his face. I shook his hand and then shook my head.

We introduced ourselves and then he walked around to the passenger side and opened the door for me – nice touch. I got in, noticing as I did that the wide and reasonably high sill was considerably easier to navigate than the (brilliant) Lotus Elise I had once owned. I nestled down into the Super Sport, noting the orange stitching heralding the car's extreme nature on the headrest. Dr Schreiber got in and we shut both the doors. This was it.

He just serenely pulled away. Gently. Quietly. Easily.

'See, Mr Roach, it's like driving a Golf . . .' he chuckled.

I doubted that very much but I appreciated Dr Schreiber trying to put my nerves at ease. We headed out on to the main road over a speed bump outside the hotel without a problem. Then it was a sharp left at some traffic lights and on to the main road towards the Autobahn. Which was where, presumably, we had to go to head to the test track.

Dr Schreiber started chatting about the car almost immediately; neither of us wanted to exchange too many pleasantries when in the presence of such a machine. It seemed inappropriate. Almost immediately I had to stop him and press 'Record' on my tape machine because quite literally every word out of his mouth fascinated me. Dr Schreiber was absolutely immaculately dressed in a pristine suit, his leather brogues shined as glossily as the Veyron's bodywork and his fingernails were trimmed, spotless and symmetrical. When he spoke, his voice was crammed with enthusiasm for the car. *Passion* again. The Veyron was a part of his life, that much was crystal clear. When I asked him a particularly

A Veyron's headroom can accomodate a man up to 6' 7" tall, or two men each 3' 3" tall.

detailed question, or when he was pondering something important, he was in the habit of placing his immaculately trimmed forefinger vertically against his top lip, where he tapped it gently in consideration, accompanied by a slight narrowing of his eyes in concentration.

I didn't dare ask if I was going to drive the car, I was too excited to just be in it.

For the first ten minutes we drove steadily along the road at around 50mph. The engine was beautifully quiet; we were just one car of many in the traffic. Nothing spectacular. Then we turned on to the Autobahn. After some more chat and as we were cruising along effortlessly at around 80mph Dr Schreiber said, 'And now I will show you a little of what the Veyron can do . . .'

I don't know what happened next, but at the time I thought we'd been hit from behind by a speeding oil tanker out of control at 150mph. My head was slammed into the headrest and my tape machine flew into the footwell. After a second or so I realised that Dr Schreiber had simply accelerated. I strained my neck against the g-forces and looked at the speedo. 150mph. It had been maybe three seconds. Was this possible?

Dr Schreiber apologised for knocking my tape machine into the footwell and laughed. I laughed too, nervously, excitedly, bewildered. He gunned it a couple of times more – with a warning first – and it began to dawn on me that I was sitting in something that was simply *extraordinary*.

'This car has two completely different souls,' explained Dr Schreiber, completely relaxed, 'two different hearts . . . It is Dr Jekyll and Mr Hyde.' Then without warning he said, 'The Veyron is also very strong at braking too, Mr Roach,' before slamming on the anchors at 140mph. Bowels turned again, neck flung forward, tape machine back in the footwell (it was a majestically stitched and fully carpeted footwell, I noted).

'It is very complicated to explain the Veyron by talking,' continued the cool and calm Dr Schreiber. 'That was the main reason why I said it would be better if you could arrange to come to Wolfsburg and we could drive in the car together because *this* is Bugatti' (he patted the luxurious steering wheel), 'this is the reason why people are interested in the car. Not the price, not the exclusivity, the main point is the car. It is *extreme*. It is difficult to imagine if you haven't been in the car yourself.' Then, with a straight face, he asked me, 'Do you have some more time, Mr Roach?'

'I have got all the time in the world, Dr Schreiber, trust me . . .'

He said he wanted to show me the car on the Autobahn for those mind-bending speeds, and revealed that the team – including himself on multiple occasions – had tested the prototypes on the public motorway itself. But he explained he was also anxious for me to see it driving around the quaint villages

Dr Wolfgang Schreiber, Chief Engineer of the Bugatti Veyron, and my companion for the Super Sport test drive.

in the more rural areas, in town, on B-roads, the full range of driving experiences. Dr Schreiber then proceeded to drive me around in the Veyron for about ninety minutes as we chatted non-stop about the car, his role in its creation, the challenges and the joys. Then he said the words I'd been anxiously awaiting for.

'So, Mr Roach, I will pull over and then would you like to have a turn?'

'Is that honestly a question that requires an answer, Dr Schreiber?' was all I could think to say. *We must be close to the test track*, I thought.

One minute later Dr Schreiber pulled over in a pine forest and onto a picnic area. *Crap, no test track, then* . . . Remember, it had been −5°C for three days and the roads were still cluttered with remnants of snow, ploughed into neat columns like ten-pin bowling guards along the side of the tarmac. He parked the Veyron and I opened the door to get out. It was then that I noticed he'd parked it on a sheet of thick black ice. The entire car park was an ice rink.

'Do you think it would be a good idea for you to pull away on to the tarmac for me, Dr Schreiber?' I asked hopefully.

'No, no need, Mr Roach. The Veyron will be fine, you'll see. It's just like a Golf.'

OK, so you are going to have to pull away in a 1200bhp car on a sheet of ice without looking like a total plank . . .

I sat in and put my seat belt on. No five-point harness, just a seat belt. I pulled the door shut, no piece of wire, just a finely machined door handle. I put the key in its slot (it's a standard switchblade key save for the Bugatti logo) and then waited while the car sent fuel and fluids surging around the complex machinery hidden so close behind my head. Then I pressed the 'Start' button and heard the slight whirr of a starter motor before the engine roared into life. A sharp intake of breath and then gently – I don't mind saying *very gently* – I pushed the accelerator pedal down.

The Veyron pulled off the ice as easily as if it was sliding along the world's most perfect tarmac. No wheel spin, no stalling, nothing. It just pulled away. That had nothing to do with any expertise on my part, all I did was gently push the accelerator down and turn the wheel. I recalled that I'd read somewhere the car can detect if you are on ice or snow. Thank God.

Relieved, I pulled out left on to the forest road and drove off, listening to Dr Schreiber telling me again how it was really 'just like a Golf, you see . . .' At this point, it was hard to disagree with him. The Veyron really does drive exactly like your own 'normal' car at low speeds. It didn't feel big, it certainly didn't feel anywhere near the two tons that it is, and the restricted visibility that I'd read about in the standard model was fine in the Super Sport as the A columns had been moved, they were there in the field of vision but no more than most cars. It wasn't an issue.

Having said that, after about two minutes of my driving, Dr Schreiber did have to tell me – a little nervously perhaps – that I was 'a little close to the ditch Mr Roach'. Left-hand drive and all that.

As we continued our chat, we approached a quaint German village which had a somewhat bone-shaking cobbled road, but the ride was no more uncomfortable than in most cars. Dr Schreiber commented on the ride being a little bumpy but I suspect mostly to reassure himself that we weren't causing thousands of pounds' worth of damage to his pristine suspension. He took the opportunity to tell me how the Veyron's suspension was in fact much softer than many super sports cars, and explained the pros and cons of hard versus softer suspension, including a sentence that contained the words 'longitudinal distribution of torque and power' and 'transverse and lateral' but, frankly, because I was driving a £2 million car around a cobbled German hamlet with traffic coming both ways on a road just about wide enough to accommodate a shopping trolley, his engineering gem of a quote went in one ear and straight out of the other. I tried to listen again when we'd exited that narrow road but as we did, a light came on next to the speedo accompanied by a shrill beep. 'Oh, this is nothing,' said Dr Schreiber, 'this is just the car telling us the outside temperature is freezing and it could be dangerous driving around, that's all.' Oh, that's all right then, I felt much better for that.

We came across a diversion so Dr Schreiber decided we should perform a three-point turn. As I popped the car into reverse, a mini-TV screen appeared in the rear-view mirror. 'This gives our customers the chance to avoid any damage. Our customers are very proud and they would blame themselves for damaging the car. This helps them to keep cool. Same with the automatic transmission,

The rear-view mirror system which contains the rear-parking camera also houses the sat-nav and numerous other functions.

it prevents you making mistakes when you take off in front of a crowded place. That is something our customers mentioned, they wanted true ease of use. It is not necessary to have a race driver's licence to drive this car. You feel safe and you feel comfortable, you can do everything, that is one of the secrets of the Veyron, the combination of both.' He wasn't kidding; he later revealed to me that on one occasion he took the Veyron test vehicle to a McDonald's drive-through, to convince himself of this 'ease of use' criteria.

The village was really *very* bumpy but Dr Schreiber seemed not to mind too much. 'This reminds me of a funny story,' he continued. 'I was in Pasadena and our sales guys had arranged some test drives for customers and one guy asked, "Is it possible to go to my house?" When we reached his home, he said, "Can we drive to the entrance and behind my house?" so I did that. Then he told me why. He had previously bought a Porsche GT but only after he'd taken delivery did he find that he couldn't get to the parking space behind his house because of the bump at the entrance, so he had to park the car in the public road. That was the reason why he sold the car after only a few months. After I parked the Veyron in his private space behind his house, he said, "This is the car for me!" and that same evening he signed the contract for a Veyron.'

We eventually pulled back out of the village and I noticed a stream of cars on the horizon, fast, ant-like. The Autobahn. My heart rate went up, again. I pulled on to the motorway and noticed the temperature gauge as we did: +2 degrees. Almost balmy.

I pulled into the traffic and quickly headed out to the fast lane, unavoidably noticing the staring eyes of every neighbouring driver as I went past. Dr Schreiber knew why I was getting out there, I knew why I was getting out there, so as soon as I was in the fast lane and there was no traffic in front of me for about forty-five miles, I did it.

I slammed my foot down in a Bugatti Veyron Super Sport.

The acceleration when you are a passenger is brutal, indescribable, joyous, adrenaline-fuelled, insane. When you are the driver it is all of those things times 1200bhp. It is genuinely *shocking*. I glanced down at the speedo – 225km/h. What? That's 140mph. I had hardly touched the pedal. I certainly hadn't gunned it. The steering was rock solid, the car was so firmly planted on the road that it was as good as on rails. It was all so . . . *deceptive*. One of my friends had said to me that the first word out of my mouth when I first pushed that beautifully machined Bugatti accelerator pedal down would be a swear word. He was right.

When you press that pedal down, the W16 engine does indeed switch personality. Dr Schreiber had warned me about Mr Hyde and he wasn't lying. Aurally it is a magnificent noise, a cacophony, an aural assault . . . I've read some purists complain that it's not a V8 or that it doesn't purr like a Ferrari. But you know what? On that Autobahn on that day at 140mph, it was just about the most perfect thing I'd ever heard. Maybe that's not a 'cool' thing to say but I'm telling it like it is. What a sound!

At one point I asked Dr Schreiber about the decision to switch from the W18 to W16 engine, but on playing the tape back I cannot make out a single syllable of what he said because the W16 is roaring into life in the background as I accelerate again and again. Never before have I been so pleased to have 'lost' part of an interview. It was almost as if the W16 was personally shouting down its predecessor, consigning it to the Veyron's garbage.

He later told me, 'When I came to Bugatti they had a flap in the exhaust system and I said, "No! This car doesn't need any flaps! No fake." This is a Bugatti Veyron, *everything* is pure, so we took the flaps away. That sound is absolutely real, it's just air flowing through the engine and coming through the outlets of the exhaust system, nothing else. We need that volume for the amount of gas to get out and this is what produces that sound.'

The most brutal acceleration is reserved for when you use the paddles on the steering wheel and drop the car back a gear (or two if you're brave/senseless) before slamming the accelerator pedal down. I tried it a few times. It's like taking off; as we know, the Veyron's top speed is faster than Concorde on take-off and when I used the paddle shift to leap forward, I had no doubt that was true. For the more sedate customer, the automatic mode is seamless and that's what I found myself using most of the time.

I was jolted back into reality when we were funnelled along into a two-lane

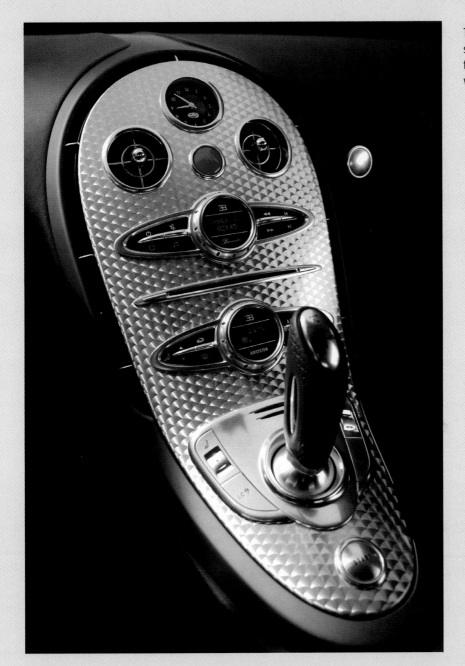

The leather-clad oblong gear shift allows access to that famous DSG gearbox in its various modes.

stretch of road with concrete blocks either side, with dozens of lorries close on my right. I admit I wasn't concentrating, I didn't see the signs, so I was still doing 100mph when I suddenly noticed that we were then going down into one lane. Time to test out those famed Veyron brakes. Sharpish.

We probably wouldn't have stopped any quicker if we'd actually hit the concrete central reservation. My neck hurt again, not for the last time that day. The brakes are completely different from anything else I've ever experienced. Not the oversized ceramic discs per se, but that amazing rear wing. It works so powerfully from behind you that it feels more like you are in some kind of reverse bungee; it's hard to explain but you don't feel like you are braking as much as actually being flung backwards. When Dr Schreiber was driving I kept looking out of the rear window (over that gloriously machined W16 piece of art) and there was the wing, twitching, rising, sinking, working silently all the time. It was almost like the hand of the father who is teaching his kid to ride a bike and 'promises' that he wasn't holding the back of the seat. When we stopped so abruptly alongside that juggernaut siphoning down into one lane, I'd like to think it was all my own work but I know deep down it wasn't, I was just along for the ride.

As we headed back to Wolfsburg I was delighted to find myself in a traffic jam. Delighted for two reasons – firstly, it meant I could steal some extra minutes in the Veyron, however slow they were; and secondly, because it proved beyond a shadow of a doubt that this is a car you can *genuinely* use every day. We were stop-start for fifteen minutes and it was a breeze. No aching clutch leg, no burning shoulders or backache. We just queued like everyone else. Of course, you might not think the Veyron was the world's most appropriate commuter's car, for a variety of reasons, but the point is it can be done. Dr Schreiber must have read my mind because it was during the slow crawl into Wolfsburg that he informed me they have a customer in Hamburg who commutes every day in his 16.4.

Sadly, after nearly two hours driving the Super Sport, I had to hand over the keys shortly after we came out of the traffic jam, so I filtered off into a service station area and parked in a lay-by next to a Transit van. After chatting for a few moments I suddenly heard a quiet 'ssshhhh', then a pause and then 'ssshhhhh'.

'What's that?' I asked. Dr Schreiber explained that when they built the rear wing, there had been two requirements – to lower it when stationary and to do so slowly. Firstly, Dr Schreiber explained that the car was designed with a smooth, curved rear and not with an abrupt air wing protruding. 'So, when you come out in the morning to drive the car again, it should look like the car that you bought, not like someone else has been driving it while you were asleep.' Secondly, they had been worried that if the wing receded quickly and a child was around the back of the car, their fingers could easily get caught and badly damaged. So, the logic was applied that if they retracted the wing in slow increments, any child would easily be able to keep their hands safe. This is the sort of mind-boggling detail that Bugatti have injected into every element of the Veyron. An air brake was needed because no conventional ceramic disc for the road could be relied upon to stop the car from speeds in excess of 250mph and to assist with the constant ebb and flow of grip versus speed at the ferocious speeds that the engine was capable of; so they produced a retractable wing that generates as much braking force as a basic VW Polo. But they also made sure they didn't hurt any little ones' fingers and, above all, they made it look bloody good too.

Sitting there with the adrenaline still coursing through me, I tried to take

400

500

600

700

800

1000

0417

km

1200

Power/PS

in the Super Sport's cockpit. Dr Schreiber explained the philosophy behind the simplistic cabin as he opened and closed the smooth glove box and tested the various knobs and buttons for me: 'You must feel all these things and then you will understand more the philosophy of the Veyron. We tried to be very focused, not to break this philosophy in any part of the car, in any function of the car; all these functions must be *logical*. The radio is logical and easy to use. Another example, rain sensors control many new cars' windscreen wipers, but sometimes in very heavy rain they are unreliable; I decided this is not for Bugatti, this is not stable enough, so we have normal functionality in the wiper arm, just four simple settings.'

He was right about the philosophy. The cabin was simple, understated, refined – albeit a little more 'sporty' in feel than the photos I'd seen of the standard 16.4 Veyron. Each headrest had those words 'Super Sport' embroidered in orange on the plush black leather (you will also find them on either side of the central console too). In the centre between the seats is that curvaceous EB logo in silver. The central control panel is really rather sparse but I liked that, I was fearful of being bemused by instruments when all I really wanted to do was drive. The $30,000 stereo system in the Super Sport is made by Bugatti and called the Puccini (the standard Veyron has a system made by Burmeister); the stereo is controlled by a simple wheel, likewise the air-con, plus there's an analogue clock and twin air vents. There are three mightily intimidating buttons: behind the gear lever is one labelled 'Start Engine' (OK), to the right of that is a button showing a small car and an arrow for 'Handling Set Up' (if I'm feeling brave) and finally to the left of the gear lever is a button with a small flag on it, which is for 'Launch Control' (no, thank you). The steering wheel is modest, on the small side of course and proudly wearing the EB logo too. Although rather petite, the wheel still allows you to see the instrument panel easily. Working anti-clockwise from bottom right, you have five circular gauges: the speedo, then the petrol, then the large central meter for the revs, then the oil temperature gauge and finally in the bottom left and rather small compared to its significance, the bhp gauge.

The bhp gauge was the one that I found myself looking at the most often when I was actually driving the Veyron. Of course, your eye flicks to the speedo by instinct but because it was in km/h I wasn't really computing the speed I was going, to me it just looked like, 'Fast – really fast – very fast – really, really fast – you might want to slow down now', etc. But the bhp gauge was like a siren on the rocks, I couldn't stop looking at it, as soon as my right foot became heavy it spiked up instantly and brutally. The bhp monitor was amazing to watch, distracting almost; under heavy acceleration it would regularly spike to 800–900bhp – that's more than an F1 car. Dr Schreiber had alerted me to this joy when he'd first been driving me earlier on. 'You will see now we have 300 horses at 150km/h and now I push the pedal down . . . [huge roar] and now we have 800 horses, and again, now we have 1200 horses and we are doing 290km/h. And it never stops. It just pushes and pushes, goes and goes . . . it never stops . . .' (Note the way Englishmen say '1000 horsepower' but every German I met said, '1000 horses'. The imagery of the latter is far more romantic so that's what I'll stick with.)

Even these gauges were subject to exacting scrutiny: 'Some speed gauges of certain cars are very optimistic, they show you more than the car is really able to deliver. With a Veyron, what you see is what you get, that gauge was developed just for this car. It is calibrated *exactly* to within 1 per cent. This is the fastest car in the world, it is not necessary to lie.'

I'd noted how the gear changes felt almost seamless; as a passenger it was hard to notice them at all, as a driver there was only the slightest hint that the car had changed gear. 'This is a special feature of the Veyron, the double clutch,' explained Dr Schreiber. 'It's very soft, it changes gears without any interruption of acceleration. Normally you have two options: on the one hand a manual shifter but then you have the problem of the clutch pedal and the force required to change gear. Or you have an automatic gearbox, but then you have a lack of power between one gear and the other. However, with this technology you don't feel the change, you just feel the power, it shifts and it goes, it goes, it goes. It makes it more comfortable on the one hand and faster on the other. The interruption of power is minimal, the gear change takes between 100 and 150 milliseconds. That is different to other super sports cars, that is more like an airplane.'

We'd parked next to a builder's van and about three cars down was a group of young men, all in their twenties, looking over. They looked pretty tough and I suddenly remembered – for the second time that day – that I was sitting in a car costing nearly £2 million. The realisation made me feel a tad vulnerable. I suggested to Dr Schreiber that we might want to move on and he smiled and agreed. But as we pulled up alongside the staring eyes of the young crowd, the largest one of all walked towards us . . . smiled and then cupped his hand to his ear in anticipation of our roaring off. Cool as a cucumber, Dr Schreiber let the W16 roar its lungs out for him and the man applauded. His friends were busy taking photos on their phones.

You may perhaps wonder what my top speed had been? It had crossed my mind when I'd thought we'd be on a test track that this might be the only chance I'd ever get to break 200mph. I should have been prepared and worked out that in Europe this equates to 321.87km/h, because as I have already mentioned the speed gauge in the Super Sport meant little to me. I hadn't worked out the exchange rate so I was in the dark. Knowing this, I thought to myself, *I'll get to*

300km/h, that must be a lot. I think it went to 307 in the end, which I'm reliably informed is just over 190mph but I can't be sure because I found it hard to focus too precisely on the dials with lorries only two lanes to my right. I've since found out that at that speed, every time I'd looked down at the speedo and that irresistible bhp gauge for *one second*, I'd just missed nearly 300 feet of road. Sorry to revisit the analogy, but that's almost a whole football pitch.

Most of all I wanted to use 1000bhp, in terms of this car and this book, that meant far more to me than breaking the 200mph barrier. There were plenty of supercar precedents for 200mph, and let's face it I was never going to go to the car's top speed either. So that wasn't my focus. It was that 1000bhp that Bugatti had so proudly trumpeted when Dr Piëch had announced the car all those years ago in Geneva. Of course, in the Super Sport there's another 200 horses to help, so in fact the 1000 was not even taking it to the limit.

I hit 1050bhp simultaneously with my top speed of 190mph. But then, with a line of lorries to one side and a metal barrier close by on the other, enough was enough. My mind was blurred, my eyes weren't really seeing straight and, frankly, I was crapping myself. I pulled off the gas and the Veyron pulled back suddenly. I breathed in, laughed, looked at a beaming Dr Schreiber and shook my head in disbelief once again as I settled back to cruising along at conversational speed, like 120mph (the car feels very at ease around this 'cruising' speed). This is one aspect that really struck me from my test drive: the words '190mph' sound ludicrously fast, but in a Veyron, because you get up there *so* quickly and can get back down to safer speeds even more rapidly, you never feel too vulnerable. You are vulnerable, of course, that's a daft speed and if Toad of Toad Hall were to swerve out in front of you without looking it would take more than his 'Poop Poop!' to save the day. But that's just how it felt . . . oddly safe.

In hindsight, when I think of 190mph on a public road, dangerous is the word which springs to mind. And in a sense, the Veyron is a dangerous car in so much as its immense capabilities are so far ahead of the average driver that the balance is skewed. This certainly applies to me. But it felt so planted and remarkably safe at that speed that it deceived me; I'm pretty sure if I'd blistered down the Autobahn likewise in an Enzo I might have been coming home in that box after all. But this is why Bugatti equipped it with those ultra-expensive tyres, the rock-solid monocoque, the safety features, that rear-wing brake. They knew they were unleashing a monster, but they also knew they had to put it on a lead.

I'd found myself pumping the accelerator regularly, it was so addictive. Dr Schreiber would be explaining something in fine detail to me and I'd be fascinated by his words, then this overwhelming urge to push the pedal down again and feel that power would come over me; it was like some kind of drag-racing Tourette's, I couldn't help myself. The problem is, in a Veyron, when you twitch your foot down at 80mph you are doing 150mph in a few blinks of an eye, so it isn't exactly the safest way of driving. But I honestly couldn't help myself. It was so addictive. If I owned a Veyron I wouldn't be able to drive it, not because of the cost but because I'd have more points on my licence than anyone in history.

I was, of course, mightily impressed by how insanely fast the Veyron goes; yet actually, I was equally impressed by how *slow* it goes. This is clearly a car you could go to the shops in. A businessman friend of mine had once owned an F1 and phoned me one day to say, 'Mart, my dad's gone to Sainsbury's in the McLaren.' I was impressed by his practicality but mostly surprised by the fact he could drive the F1 around a Sainsbury's car park at all. The Veyron is not like that. Anyone can drive it, literally. You might not be able to pick up much shopping in the front boot, which can only accommodate a couple of bags of 'Basics' apples or similar. But methinks most Veyron owners probably don't spend much of their lives waiting in a queue for a free till at Asda.

So I had finished my drive in the Super Sport and the time had come to give the keys back to Dr Schreiber. I felt like Gollum handing over the One Ring; there was a definite primeval reluctance to hand over the shiny metal object, and I did so almost in slow motion, with Dr Schreiber having to give a definite tug on my grip to set them free. As I sat back down in the passenger seat, I felt decidedly melancholy. I recalled the words of Jeremy Clarkson after he'd driven the Veyron for the first time on *Top Gear*, when he'd raced the Bugatti across Europe against James May's Cessna light aeroplane, and now I completely understood that he hadn't been playing up to the camera when he said, 'I've got to go for the rest of my life knowing that I'll never own that car.' Like Clarkson, I wanted to drive the Veyron again straight away. Just as the acceleration spike is instantly addictive, like an automotive equivalent of lethal crack cocaine, so was the overall experience. Maybe I could ask for a Big Mac at that drive-through, and while Dr Schreiber was inside washing his hands I could 'hold the keys' for him . . . *No, no. Stop it, my Precious.*

IN THE FURNACE OF THE BEAST

D r Schreiber drove us back through the urban streets around Wolfsburg and then he pulled left into the entry for a petrol station. Except in true Area 51 style, we drove round the back of the petrol station and pulled up to a high metal fence with a security guard and traffic barrier. A quick nod to the guard from Dr Schreiber gave us instant access and the metal barrier lifted to allow us through. We drove into what looked like a normal car park – except it wasn't a normal car park because alongside the VWs and the odd Audi was a Veyron convertible Grand Sport. Next to the handful of cars was a square, low-rise and fairly nondescript office block: Bugatti.

Parking in the space right next to the glass entrance door, we got out but instead turned right and away from the reception area. *Perhaps he can't actually take me inside*, I thought. 'You will like it over here instead,' said Dr Schreiber as he walked across the car park to what looked like a store room and pulled its metal door open.

I walked in to be confronted by no fewer than five Bugatti Veyrons, all in various states of undress. It's quite a shock seeing over £5 million worth of cars in a workshop about fifty feet long (with 'my' Super Sport and that Grand Sport parked just outside too). Dr Schreiber pointed at another orange and black Super Sport just inside the doorway and said, 'This is the sister car to your one, this is the world record holder . . .'

So this was the 267mph car. This was the Veyron that *Top Gear*'s James May had driven to what was at the time a record of 259mph, only for Bugatti's test driver Pierre-Henri Raphanel to snatch it away from him moments later with the record-breaking run. For the briefest of times, Captain Slow was the fastest driver on earth. Looking at the car, identical to the one I'd been driving that afternoon, the basic premise behind my quest hit me full in the face, as brutally as the Veyron's acceleration: here was a *celebrity*. No doubt about it.

Looking at that car was exhilarating: this was the actual vehicle that had broken the world speed record for a production car. To see it now in the context of a completely normal workshop was very peculiar. You get used to seeing professional photographs of supercars whizzing around some Californian coastal

After a week of the world's press hammering several Veyrons at its Sicily launch, only one set of brake pads had to be changed.

road or a glistening and beautifully lit studio shot. Here, among the oil cans and numerous instruments and racks, it almost . . . I say *almost* . . . looked like a normal car.

As we stood in the workshop next to the five Bugattis, Dr Schreiber walked around each one in turn and explained what he was looking at and what it reminded him of from the development days. As I started to walk around the clutch of Veyrons, the door to the workshop opened and a tall man walked in and waved. He introduced himself as Herr Schnell and chatted briefly with Dr Schreiber in German. Dr Schreiber then said, 'Herr Schnell was responsible for the engine application.' That's all 1001bhp. The brilliantly named Mr Fast must be the most smug man in the car world? Not so. 'Ah yes, that was me, but I'm also responsible for the emissions, sorry about that.' Ten minutes later another man walked in and breezed over, again a slither of German was shared before he was also introduced. 'This is Herr Hasselmeyer, he was responsible for overseeing the overriding development progress'. 'Well, what I actually did was all the bits that no one else wanted to do.' Such engineering brilliance coated in a layer of humility. Unexpected.

The most fascinating Veyron in there, even including James May's celebrity in the corner, was the one with almost no bodywork on it at all, sitting alone like a complex insectoid robot. 'See how tight this car has to be built?' said Dr Schreiber as we approached and, boy, was he right. To a non-mechanical mind such as mine, the back of a Bugatti Veyron looks exactly like the rear view of Doc Brown's DeLorean DMC-12 in *Back to the Future* (which I'd seen in the flesh only the day before at the Autostadt). In the film, the madcap professor had modified his car so much that the guts had spilled out over the rear bodywork like some disembowelled spaceship. Here there seemed to be even more internal mechanisms, only Bugatti somehow fitted all of this under the sleek curves of that beautiful body shape. How? It didn't seem possible. I gestured towards Dr Schreiber by raising my knee and forcing some imaginary piece of engine down to fit in. He laughed. I suspect I wasn't far from the truth. There is not a spare centimetre underneath the bodywork of a Veyron. 'The car is so tight; everything has functionality, there is nothing which is just a gimmick. We have no space for that. Usually when you are developing a car, you can often see solutions in other vehicles and maybe use that idea for your project. But with the Veyron, you cannot do that because you have no space for [using ideas from] other cars. That forced us to find our own unique solutions in many, many things. The engine dimensions are more or less the same as the whole car.' This remarkable tightness under the skin also means the mighty W16 engine is just 40cm from the back of your head in the cabin. And what proportion of those parts in a Veyron were created and made solely for that car? 'About 95 per cent,' replied Dr

Schreiber without hesitation. He then continued to point out numerous parts of the stripped-back masterpiece in front of us, although he neglected to show me where the 'flux capacitor' was. *That's probably top secret*, I thought.

Next to the Veyron that had been skinned was a standard 16.4, which at first glance looked a little tired. That's because it was. 'This,' said Dr Schreiber, with genuine affection in his voice, 'is the first ever Veyron built just prior to the actual production run.' He explained that by 'first ever' he meant the first ever test model built using parts that were selected from an original production parts list. Although I'd been bowled over by James May's Super Sport, which was a historically important car standing just a few feet away, part of me couldn't help thinking that perhaps this battered specimen was actually the star of the show. 'This is the car of the Bugatti engineers!' smiled Dr Schreiber. 'They are proud of this car. I think Bugatti will never sell this car.'

We switched the ignition on: 102,263 kilometres on the clock. The dashboard's leather was mangled, damaged with scuff and tear marks where various instruments had been attached to it for development and research purposes at some point. Behind the passenger's seat was a tumble of wires and pieces of plastic, spilled out unceremoniously in mid-investigation like it had been drawn and quartered by the engineers. The leather of the steering wheel was worn, a patina that can only come through being driven for mile after mile after mile. The wheels were chipped and exhausted-looking. It had clearly been through the mill. And the licence plate: BS WS 612. BS stands for Braunschweig; WS stands for Wolfgang Schreiber ('I am very proud of that!' he smiled); and all the cars with a six at the beginning are series production cars.

That chief test car clearly begged the question: 'How many parts have you had to replace on this?' I suspected that it was essentially a new car, cannibalised from the original and rebuilt entirely many times over. Dr Schreiber tapped his top lip again, 'Erm, not many, it is the original gearbox, same for the engine, a few parts for wear and tear but not much else.' So, this thing is reliable as well. (Several weeks later, I emailed Dr Schreiber to ask how much it would cost to replace an engine or a clutch; after some days of investigating for me, he eventually wrote back and said they'd never had to do it).

The Veyron's curvaceous lines are not entirely typical of many supercars, which often have – particularly in the past – been very angular and abrupt. Even the mighty Dr Piëch had previously been very honest about Bugatti's own design history when talking to writer Herbert Völker for his book. *Marque, Legend, Renaissance*: 'Bugatti and design is a subtle and difficult topic. There were some beautiful cars in the classic period but any number of ugly ones too.' Dr Schreiber himself describes the Veyron's lines as a 'female note' and it's true that the Veyron's design language is not as masculine as some of its contemporaries.

Eric Gallina, Editor of *Car Design News* has this to say about the Veyron's shape: 'There are attributes besides its aesthetic that are particularly interesting. It's about technological advancement but it blends those functional points with an uncompromised aesthetic. The design is quite unique in the supercar category. They still retained the classic elements of the brand such as the horseshoe grille which makes it a unique front end, almost brutish, squared off. That is not what you would normally see for aerodynamic functionality and efficiency.

Eric Gallina: 'Everything was built around functionality. Look at the shoulder line of the car, for example. Everything falls into that air intake to cool that massive engine. It's a small car but it has that presence, that stance, dictated by the long wheel-base because they needed to keep the car planted. It's a rather romantic shape, definitely voluptuous'.

It's important to remember when discussing the development of the car with him that the shape is something he *inherited*, Herr Warkuss's stunning design being his starting point. 'The car was shown to many people at motor shows and so on,' he explained. 'The customer was convinced about the shape, they liked this so it was an additional risk for Bugatti to modify that when we developed the car ready for production. So one key point was to leave the shape as it was at the beginning and to find a way of bringing air in, bringing air out, bringing all these many, many parts which you need to create a Veyron underneath this body. This was much more difficult for us. We had different goals: we had super sports car goals but to leave the shape like it was at the beginning made it all the more complicated. However I think this was the right way. We were made to look for many, many special solutions for different technical problems, rather than by doing normal things. It was right to do that. It gave the brand its spirit back. Now Bugatti is alive again.'

I asked him for some examples and he mentioned the bonnet, sitting proud as it does of the side panels: 'This came out of the styling items. I am not a stylist but they wanted it to look lighter, not rigid and fixed with the car, so raising it like this gives a sense of lightness. The bonnet being like that was totally a styling point, it was nothing to do with the engineers.'

I asked him what other aspects of engineering had been required to fit in

with the body and overall styling that had been inherited. He laughed with a good-hearted snort of breath, smiled widely and began to detail many elements of that gorgeous bodywork that had landed his team with a major engineering headache. 'I will be here all day, but this is a good example,' he said, and went on to explain that the early development cars had a large cutaway in the side of the door, near where the panel meets the front fender. This was inserted because the assumption was made that the car would need to get prodigious amounts of hot air away from its front end and in particular the brakes.

'The first prototypes in the stage-two cars had a hole in the door here,' explained Dr Schreiber, 'and some engineers said this is absolutely necessary to have this hole otherwise we cannot bring the hot air out of the brakes area and out of the radiator there. But Dr Piëch said, "No, I don't like that hole." So we modified one door without a hole and measured the resulting heat in a wind tunnel, the question being, "Is it really true that air goes out of that cutaway hole and has such a cooling effect on the radiators and the aerodynamics?" Yet after our experiment and various measurements, we found there was no real influence. So we did away with the hole. That was maybe the most critical point from the styling side. The big boss didn't want the hole; the engineers said, "We need the hole." The first production car? No hole.'

Because of the fixed shape, innovative and state-of-the-art technology had

A symbol of the Veyron's stylistic emphasis – the door cut-away that was discarded on Piëch's insistence to be used to improve aerodynamics. The undercarriage was streamlined and included so-called venturi-shaped channels which funnel the air and help to increase downforce. The impressive silver pods on the back of the standard Veyron are not part of the aero package, but are in fact coolers, although there is an obvious and very pleasing aesthetic element to them too.

Another example was the materials used for the door itself. The shape was set without the hole, but the stylists also wanted it made from aluminium so that it had a 'solid' and rewarding feeling and sound when opened and closed by the customer. However, the actual shape of the door proved very difficult to make in aluminium (as against carbon fibre, which is used on the majority of the bodywork). 'So we needed to create a special technique for producing these deep doors and fenders out of aluminium. And round the back here, the panels next to the engine block were creating glare for the driver's rear mirror, so we had to produce a special matt finish on those two panels to eliminate this. Again because we couldn't change the shape.'

Then I asked Dr Schreiber the same question in reverse. 'What elements of styling had to be compromised to fit in with an engineering necessity?' He muttered, 'Hmmmm, let me think,' then out came his forefinger again, gently tapping his top lip in contemplation. He walked around the car, silently pondering for well over two minutes. Then he looked up and said, 'No, none, nothing.'

As we'd strolled around each Veyron in the workshop in turn, dissecting its inner workings, what fascinated me talking to Dr Schreiber at that point was the amount of times he said, 'So it was back to the drawing board,' or 'So we had to go back and start over . . .' Yet each time he said this, there was no sense of frustration, no anger – maybe this was because we were talking in retrospect, they'd achieved their goal; had I interviewed Dr Schreiber during the turbulent development itself, I might have found a decidedly more frazzled team. But I think not. Dr Schreiber's quiet confidence was all-consuming.

Next we walked into the spares department. It looked like the store room of a hardware shop, rack after rack of spares in matching boxes, with about ten aisles of treasure, all organised and neatly labelled. As we continued the tour I noticed car jacks with Bugatti's logo on them, the same as on numerous other toolboxes I'd seen. 'They are very proud to work on Bugattis,' explained Dr Schreiber, when I pointed this out. Another treat was an engine block sitting alone in a room sectioned off from the main workshop, silent, massive, its four turbos naked and exposed.

Next to 'the world's most expensive parts shop' was a tyre 'corner', scaffolded shelves with the Veyron's rubbers in piles of rear and front. On first glance it looked like a Kwik Fit, but then when you actually looked again, it was anything but. Only when they are taken off the car and set aside like this can you truly

understand how *massive* the Veyron's tyres are. Below the tall columns of gigantic rubber there was a single tyre on the floor, laid flat, so I walked up to it and put my leg against it. It came nearly up to my knee (and I'm six foot). 'And do you want to see the bigger rear one?' asked Dr Schreiber. 'You're kidding, right?' He wasn't, the rear tyre is gargantuan. *Well, if I get thrown out of my hotel, I can climb inside a tyre and at least have somewhere to sleep . . .* This also explained why there'd been (only slightly) restricted leg room in the footwell of the Super Sport, to accommodate such massive rubbers.

The tyres are this big for a good reason: to safely hold a car of this weight on the road at 250mph+. As I have noted, they had to be developed by Michelin with the Veyron specifically in mind. The main issue was their robustness and performance when operating at the top speeds that the car was capable of. Again, journalists had queried whether conventional tyres could withstand the enormous pressures and demands at such a road speed. But Michelin had come up trumps in both a technical and *literally* big way. In fact, the tyre will actually run safely to 280mph.

Eventually we locked up the workshop and switched the lights off on those five remarkable cars, then walked a short stroll across the car park, past the

These high-speed tyres are indeed designed exclusively for the Veyron. The fronts are coded 265-68 R 500 A and the rear as 365-71 R 540. In addition, due to the risks of such high speed stresses, the tyres and wheels incorporate the innovative PAX System which reacts to – and therefore accommodates safely – sudden pressure loss.

Michelin developed the tyres at their research and test facility at Clermont-Ferrand. Each tyre consists of multiple layers of rubber. According to *National Geographic*, a standard car tyre takes thirty seconds to make; a hand-made Veyron tyre takes more than one hour.

Grand Sport and my Super Sport, to the office building adjacent to the workshop in the fortified compound. On reception was an immaculate woman who greeted us with a warm smile. We walked to the first floor and Dr Schreiber took me into his former office, where Mr Dirk Isgen, Bugatti's new chief of engineering, now resides. The office was modest, perhaps only fifteen feet square, with a simple desk on one side resting opposite a table with ten black chairs around it. In the middle of the table was a half-empty bottle of water next to a newspaper clipping about the new Golf, as well as some technical drawings. This was where the various heads of the Veyron team would regularly congregate. I could easily picture those ten expansive brains sitting around this table mulling over technical challenge after technical challenge. My mind flicked to the similarly close-knit and small design team that the brand founder Ettore Bugatti had been so proud of . . . ghosts of challenges past? Maybe.

I asked Dr Schreiber if the heritage of Bugatti had been an influence. 'I had the chance to drive in a Type 35 in Wolfsburg and that was really a very strange feeling for me. It was fun on the one hand, but if I am honest, I always think when I look at these old cars that, OK, if you want to improve things, you cannot find the solution in these old cars. That is not possible. We must go a different way, find new solutions, so it doesn't really help me in my work. I am not an enthusiast concerning historic cars, that is not my passion.'

However, there was clearly a shared approach: 'I was impressed by Ettore's incredible achievements in these early stages of motor history. I never met him, unfortunately, but I am convinced he was a very good engineer, not only a visionary but also a good engineer. When I see these old cars, they are very well

'My' Super Sport parked up at the Bugatti compound; note the Grand Sport in the background.

made. He created very clever solutions, and they also had the intention not to do anything just as a gimmick, to concentrate on the function. We say "Form, Technique, Function" must be combined in every Bugatti car. That is also found in these old cars.'

As we strolled out of his former office, Dr Schreiber pointed out that there was not one single exactly rectangular corner in the entire building. Looking at the walls, I could see he was right, even the coving on the ceiling was specially rounded. He even opened the door to the gents toilets and pointed out the unusual curved layout. The architect had intended this to maximise the feng shui and positive atmosphere in the office building. Who was to say it hadn't worked rather well?

We sat at a table near a large window overlooking the nearby petrol station and road. I was bursting with yet more questions for Dr Schreiber, about the development of the car, the infamous delays, the technical issues, the challenges. It was time to get oily hands again. There was only one place to start: 'Is it true – or was it just PR spin – that Dr Piëch had requested a car that could be driven to the opera?'

'This is absolutely true,' explained Dr Schreiber. 'When I came to Bugatti from VW's transmission development department, it was normal business to have some papers where everything was exactly written down concerning the power, the torque, everything about the car would be described, prior to the first prototype. But at Bugatti they already had the first prototypes so I asked, "What is our description of the car? What will it *be* when it is ready?" Dr Piëch just said these four things. "A car with 1001 horses. A car that is able to accelerate faster than three seconds from zero to 100. A car that is able to reach a top speed of 406km/h. And a car in which the customer is able to drive in front of an opera house on the same day as using the other three assets." That was everything, that was the brief, the basis for this car.

'Now prior to me [coming to the project] they had big, big problems fulfilling the first targets: the power, the top speed and the acceleration were big challenges. Plus, we had to leave the shape like it was in the first stages and combine it with all these sports-car qualities. After a while working on the Veyron, I found that we would hopefully fulfil these three requirements *but* in combination with the fourth requirement – the opera – it was clear that this would be the most advanced target for the whole car. That was the main problem.'

'And what was your very first day on the project?' I asked.

'If I remember correctly I went to the workshop and I asked my co-workers for a test drive. But that was not possible . . . we had many, many different problems in the first period of the development phase. The most critical thing was that these many problems prevented the development people working with their baby, with their car, they couldn't *drive* it. It sounds very easy but that was one of the main problems when we began, to just drive with our own cars, our own prototypes. These basic problems had nothing to do with the Veyron. Nothing to do with 1000 horses, nothing to do with the massive torque, etc. Only after we addressed these issues did I feel we had a chance to see the *real* problems, the real challenges that were necessary to fulfil all the different targets.

'For example, the car has a hydraulic system for bringing it up or down at various speeds, and in addition to that the wing is designed to come out to create more stability for higher speeds up to 360km/h. To enable the car to do that, it was necessary to implement a hydraulic system on four springs to pump it up or to let it down.'

The pre-existing hydraulic system that Dr Schreiber was talking about was miraculous yet problematic. It was capable of lifting the two-tonne car up or down – depending on speeds and aerodynamics – in *one second*. It was a masterpiece, but it was also exceptionally complicated. So the decision was taken that moving the car up or down so fast was not necessary. A slower but simpler system had to be designed. Eventually it was discovered that years previously a hydraulic system had been under development (within the group) that never made it into production. The problem was the engineers had mostly retired so Bugatti recalled them and their knowledge proved vital.

Another specific problem was that the knocking sensor on the engine didn't work. The engine had so many cylinders and so many knocking noises that the accurate detection of every single cylinder was virtually impossible. So Dr

Schreiber's team had to develop the so-called Ion Flow System to measure the electricity of the ignition spark and then decide whether there was a knocking in the cylinder or not. Such a system had never even been close to a production car before, but the team found a company that had done extensive development on this concept, so they ran some tests and found that yes, it did work.

These manifold and complex issues clearly affected morale: 'Everybody was laughing about Bugatti the brand and [the team] was in a deep depression, at least that was my feeling when I came to the project,' explained Dr Schreiber. So he and the incumbent chief executive officer Dr Paefgen decided to talk to the people already working on the project in an attempt to analyse what was causing the most problems. There was a general sense of over-complication. It was crucial that this mass of super-complex engineering challenges was quickly broken down into manageable defined and specific issues.

In fact, Dr Schreiber highlighted a whole batch of key problems that were preventing the car from being launched – some were basic, some were unique to the Veyron's ludicrous performance goals. In a later email, Dr Schreiber wrote that specifically these included (but were not limited to):

- cooling of all fluids in a very tight car (water and oil)
- tyres and rims
- transmission and driveline
- weight (200kg too much)
- central hydraulic system
- aerodynamics in each mode (standard, high speed, top speed)
- power of 1001bhp in a car – not just on a test bench
- brakes
- torsional and bending stiffness of the whole car
- power steering
- all systems for ABS, ESP, traction control etc.

The most frequently cited problem in the media had been cooling, with the mid-engine layout not helping matters (typically, a front-engine car enjoys better cooling from more direct exposure to the outside air next to the bonnet; a mid-engine car is rather more 'suffocated'). Were they right? 'Cooling was one of the major issues, yes. If an engine delivers 1000bhp for the wheels, it also produces an additional 2000bhp in heat [enough to warm 100 family homes through an entire winter]. About 1000bhp goes out to the exhaust system and 1000 goes into the cooling system. Our cooling system is able to cool about 600–650bhp completely, to a stable level of temperature. It is not possible to use more than 650bhp for [long periods] because that would overheat the cooling system but also there is no street in the world where you can do that; anyway, I have not

The Veyron's ten radiators carry 40 litres of water. Each one is made up of thirty plates, placed gently on top of one another by hand; each plate has 600 separate grooves for water to flow through. Each radiator takes 15 hours to build.

found this street.' Dr Schreiber also confirmed that the story suggesting the first few test runs of the W16 engine melted the ventilation system on the roof of the test facility was true.

So what about these fabled ten radiators? 'We looked for every space in the car for radiators, for every sensible space, that was a massive challenge.' On a superficial level, the huge cooling demands were one reason why the Veyron's boot is not exactly spacious. Only an overnight bag will fit in.

The Super Sport has its own special radiator for the rear axle oil, because of the extra power. 'For the Super Sport those 200 extra horses created more heat, so we had to find a different place for the rear axle oil and we [eventually] implemented that in the double diffuser of the car.' And of course, let's not forget that the Veyron's engine itself is exposed to the outside world, to further enhance the cooling abilities of the car – although in the flesh this is impressive as much for its aesthetics as it is for its engineering.

'It wasn't just with the engine that cooling that was an issue,' continued Dr Schreiber. 'The wheels were subjected to massive temperatures at 350km/h+ and so rigorous tests had to be completed, principally because a catastrophic wheel failure would almost certainly be fatal at such speed. Acceptable limits were set and never exceeded in tests.'

We've noted the ingenious DSG gearbox that the Veyron possesses. But behind the scenes, creating the gearbox that could handle the colossal amount of power generated by the W16 engine was a massive headache. Just as well they had Dr Schreiber on the case, then, as he is widely regarded as one of the world's leading automotive gearbox experts. 'The knowledge about DSG was coming

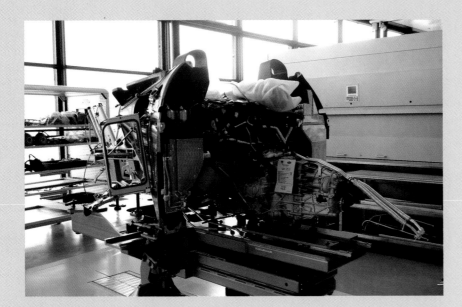

The DSG sits ahead of the engine in the Veyron.

from VW because that was what I brought with me into the project. I was, how do you say it? . . . the "father" of the DSG and I thought that system was perfect for the Veyron, exactly what we needed. The first prototypes had no DSG, they had an automatic manual shifter, but Dr Neumann, the former chief of Bugatti, asked me whether in my opinion it was correct to stay with the automatic manual when we knew we were making a Golf in a very short time that would have a technically better transmission. I advised him to change to DSG because if Golfs and Audi A3s have better technical gearboxes than the most powerful super sports car in the world, then we have a problem. So they changed to the DSG technology very shortly before I came to the project. Then we optimised it and step by step we found a way to make it more or less perfect.'

Another issue had been the weight; Bugatti purists noted that the company's founder Ettore despised heavy vehicles, hailing the edict that 'weight was the enemy'. When Dr Schreiber had first come to the struggling project, the car was 200kg overweight. Dozens of parts were re-examined and redesigned in lighter materials: the exhaust, axle springs, brake disc hats and heat shields, valve and intercooler covers for example, and special aluminium alloys were created for use in very thin components like radiator hoses, wings and doors. Even the onboard electronics systems were ripped out and comprehensively redesigned using special lightweight cabling previously only used in aircraft and racing cars. The various lightweight construction techniques employed resulted in a total weight saving of almost 200kg.

Even so, Dr Schreiber has no truck with the weight criticisms often levelled at the Veyron. '[The media] always discussed about the weight of the car, they said a two-tonne car is not a super sports car. But that is just a figure, if you sit in the car, if you feel the car and how it steers, accelerates and drives, you get a completely different impression. You don't *feel* the two tonnes. Today, if you take into account our body weight and the fuel in the tank, we had 2.5 tonnes in that Super Sport, but I think you didn't feel like that?' He was right. 'The 4WD helps,' he continued, 'the huge torque helps, 1500Nm of torque. Good brakes, very good brakes, all these things help to give you a completely different impression. But it is not just an impression, it is real. It is a very agile and easy-to-drive car. So for me personally the weight is not that important, it is just a number.'

Perhaps not surprisingly, the sheer top speeds the car was aiming for produced some challenges, not least in the demands on parts but also in the aerodynamics. 'When we tried to drive 400km/h for the first time on the [test track's] high-speed oval, we only reached 360km/h before we found the first problem. The sealing for our drive shafts were not stable enough for this high rotation, they became bigger and bigger [as the speed increased] and then touched another part of the car and were destroyed. One problem; so we solved the problem. Take it out for a test drive again. There's another problem. The rear axle suffered problems with oil spilling out of the axle housing over certain speeds because the parts in the rear axle rotated so fast that they literally just pumped oil out all over the place. So we thought about a solution and found one. This time we mounted a small hose that ended in a cup, the idea being that if the oil was forced out, it would travel down the hose and be collected safely in the cup. A second hose then took that excess oil back to the housing. We implemented this, took it out for a test drive at over 360 and again it worked. Problem solved. Next . . .'

Even the windscreen wipers were designed to maximise aerodynamic performance at such prodigious speeds: 'We had to prevent the dangerous situation that if the customer is driving over 350 they might lose the wiper altogether. And this lip on the wiper here? It's for aerodynamics.'

Which brought me to the question: 'What was it like the first time you topped 400?'

'Well, first of all, we didn't really know if the car was really stable and capable of driving so fast. So we went to Switzerland and asked the Sauber Formula 1 team to let us use their wind tunnel, because we'd heard that it was able to manage wind speeds of 250km/h. When we were in the wind tunnel we asked those guys, "What is necessary to reach 400?" and they said, "OK, we don't know. We can give you support for speeds up to 360 . . . but 400? . . . no."'

Audi race engineers were also consulted about various aerodynamic issues. 'We knew that minor modifications of the aerodynamic parts of the car would have a huge influence, it can be huge at such speeds. We found that the angle of the rear wing in the so-called top speed configuration was crucial. If you drive

that fast, 400 or more, the configuration gives you stability to go straight at these very high speeds. Our testing told us that at 400, only one degree of difference made a substantial difference to stability. That's why it was necessary for us to implement sensors in the wing.'

In stark contrast, other factors did not have an influence. 'Take the wing mirrors, the vibrations in the glass at 400 were an [issue]. At 200km/h, some cars have problems with vibrations, but we needed to provide wing mirrors without vibrations up to 400. Aerodynamics was another concern. We tried to do this [shuts wing mirror flat to the body] when we had our test drive to reach 400 – no influence.' In the same high-speed tests, the tyre valves were starting to open from the immense centrifugal forces and a window that had inadvertently been left partially open was sucked out altogether.

OK, so you had the engineering in place to – in theory – achieve 400km/h. But what did it *feel* like when you first achieved that speed? Dr Schreiber smiled broadly as he recalled that day: 'I felt, *We are going to do this, we are going to achieve these goals*. That was about nine months before we launched the car. [At the track] we measured the speed with GPS sensors, using two different systems just in case one failed. It was a normal day in the week, not really sunny but not raining either. We had two sensors about 100 metres apart to measure the time taken [between sensors and thus calculate a speed]. We placed one member of our team on that second sensor and she called me after the car had driven past, "427! 427km/h!" and I said, "What's wrong? It cannot be! We see here only 411."

And then we investigated the [discrepancy] and found the problem which was that 100 metres was much too short to calculate such a fast speed accurately. [When we finally verified the 400+ speed] on that day, I felt that OK, we will reach the target, we are going to do this. But we still had a lot of work to do.'

By May 2005 it was widely known in car circles that the Veyron had registered a speed of 248.5mph at the Ehra-Lessien test track, as verified by the German Homologation Authority. Although ordinarily such a speed was ludicrously fast – indeed nearly 9mph faster than the long-time record holder, the McLaren F1 – in the case of the Veyron some people had actually expected considerably more!

Testing a car at such speeds was not without elements of genuine danger. 'We were in South Africa for a test drive,' explained Dr Schreiber, 'and had acquired a special licence that allowed us to drive very fast on a public road, 350+, because they have very straight roads over there. On one run, we caught a bird in the middle of the Bugatti emblem; now at that time the grille was made out of aluminium and the bird came through the mesh and damaged all three coolers, one behind the other. So we created a mesh out of titanium instead of aluminium, which proved five times as expensive.

'The next part of the story is not a lie: amazingly nine months later we were again in South Africa and again we caught a bird in the grille. This time we found that the bird was shredded but the mesh was only slightly dented, and the coolers behind were completely OK. *That's Bugatti.* That's the difference.' Bugatti had been one the first manufacturers to ever use alloy wheels (rather than wire spoked wheels), way back in the 1920s on the Type 35, so it seemed appropriate that all these decades later they were still looking to push the envelope with their construction materials.

Another problem hit Dr Schreiber when he took the Veyron out on the Autobahn one day and hit 320km/h, only to find the ESP (Electronic Stability Program) light went out. He was told that the team didn't know if the car would be stable with the system engaged above such speeds. He was not satisfied so they arranged tests in the Black Rock desert in America to test the stability system at even higher velocity. 'The Black Rock desert has dust one and a half centimetres deep, so when you drive there you need a lot of power from the rear wheels to roll the front wheels through that dust. I drove the car, the guy from Conti [who'd developed the ESP system] sat beside me and when we reached 320–330km/h without any ESP, it oversteered! I did everything to hold it on track and prevent a big problem and luckily we managed to correct the car. So now at those higher speeds we have the light on!'

Once this exhaustive development of the Bugatti Veyron was complete, the cars still had to pass the rigorous road tests that a Golf or Passat does. 'The Veyron

is very well tested,' explained Dr Schreiber. 'We created our own test procedure for the Bugatti Veyron at [the VW test track] Ehra-Lessien. All our prototypes for the VW group have to fulfil test procedures over many, many thousands of kilometres. We crash tested the Veyron too, because we had to fulfil all the normal crash-test requirements for a standard road car. In total we crashed two cars several times, including one that was crashed twelve times. After each crash test, we built those two cars up again, crashed them again and so on. The final crash is called the "offset crash" which involves both cars and after that you cannot repair the car again, they are scrapped.' Painfully, several Veyrons also suffered minor dents and knocks after a handful of smaller accidents in testing.

This all sounds expensive?

'That is right! There was also another great difficulty, we had so few prototypes. In total there were three different stages of prototypes for the Veyron. For Stage 1 cars we had four; Stage 2 cars we just had eight; and Stage 3 cars, the final stage prior to pre-production, we only had five. That was it, everything, and that is very few [by industry standards]. If you come from VW or Audi they would say it is not possible to fulfil all the requirements of so many markets with so few cars – for example the US has different crash requirements, different emissions requirements and so on. But we had very good people in our team who did nothing other than make time plans and schedules for every group of development guys: who has the car from when to when and for what purpose. These guys did nothing else other than to coordinate these prototype cars, to the nearest minute sometimes.'

Where are all these prototypes? Do they still exist?

'Not all of them, no. Some are crashed, some are just scrap because they were old and some still exist.' Was this extensive testing – aside from the legally required ones – really necessary? 'For us, yes. When I came to the project some people said to me that customers will not use the car like a normal car, they will be collectors or maybe drive it once a year. I replied that I could not imagine that, I am a car guy and I was bewildered by that statement. *Is it really true that the customers will just look at the Bugatti Veyron?* They have a car with 1000 horses and just want to look. When you look the first time, OK, it's nice, then the second time . . . OK . . . but after a while it will be boring, you will *surely* drive that car, I cannot believe otherwise. That's the reason why we created such a long-run durability test for this car at Ehra-Lessien. We also ran a seven-hour city test in Tokyo, among other tests. This all ensured that it was so reliable. We know a lot of customers with 30,000 kilometres or more on their cars.'

By now my mind was swirling with the complexity of what Dr Schreiber had been in charge of. How did he coordinate such a task? 'I am an engineer and I try to always understand every aspect of a project. Only then can I understand the problems of my co-workers and therefore *support* my co-workers. Is theirs a really big problem or is it just a normal problem that we can solve quite easily? We had many discussions in my office around the big table but most importantly of all, every evening at 8 p.m. in the workshop I just showed you, we had a meeting with everybody standing in the centre of those cars, each boss of each section of the project. And we would stand there together and discuss the daily problems, every problem, for however long it took. So the electrical guy had an impression of the problems of the engine guy. And the engine guy had an impression of the problems of the brakes guy and so on. The cars were there, so we could touch the parts, see and *feel* the problem. Those 8 o'clock discussions sometimes went on till *very* late in the night, but those meetings made us feel like such a team.'

Given all these monumental difficulties and challenges, I asked him if there was ever a moment or a day when he felt they were in a losing battle. Without hesitation, Dr Schreiber replied: 'No. I am a very optimistic human and also an engineer so I think that if people are able to fly to the moon then we should be able also to bring a car with 1000 horses into production. I never had the feeling that we would not reach that goal. After we enabled the development guys to drive the car, to work with their car, to *feel* their car and see how it worked, then they became more and more self-confident. Suddenly we had this feeling in the team of "Why not?!" Confidence is *very* important to an engineer, it's the basis for everything; if engineers are not convinced that they can reach their goal, their target, then they will not *fight*.'

This fighting spirit is one of the chief reasons why Dr Schreiber was brought to the project. The then-incumbent Bugatti CEO, Dr Paefgen – we will meet him later – had heard about this spirit and Dr Schreiber unintentionally confirmed his own reputation to me: 'When we developed the dual clutch transmission over seven years at VW, we had many, many situations where some – *most* – people said, "Stop! You will never get this to production, it's too complicated." But I

always replied, "I cannot see any real reason to stop. We will go on and solve this problem."'

'So are you stubborn or optimistic?'

'Both. First of all, as I've said, I am an optimist. I have learned over many years that nothing costs less than *thinking* about a problem. I haven't seen any problem in twenty-six years which is not reachable, not solvable somehow. Often people stop too early and say it is not worth reaching the [solution], but from my character, my personality, I am an optimist. On the other hand, *I cannot accept* that we will find no way out of a problem, out of a particular situation. That's pure stubbornness. So a combination of both, I guess.'

Obviously, given that I am writing this book, I feel that the Veyron is *special*, it's not just any supercar. This might seem partisan, but I wanted to directly ask Dr Schreiber this question: 'When – if ever – did you feel that you and your team were creating something special?'

'When I saw the car the first time before I worked on the project, I immediately got the impression that it was a special car. The look, the data, the power, the sound of the engine, all these made it special for me. During the development phase I had a chance to see everything and find every one of its secrets – that chance to create this car together with all the other guys was amazing, and so I was convinced from the beginning it was a completely special car. I didn't need any journalists to tell me that.

'But there was one specific moment when I realised that it really was something out of the ordinary. Not long before we launched the car, Ferrari phoned me up to ask if I could supply them with a Golf with DSG, because they couldn't buy one in the short time-frame they had for a certain development project they were working on. They openly told me they had the intention of analysing the DSG for their own benefit. So I said, "Yes, I have one that I can loan to you, but what can we get in return?"

'They said, "What do you want?"

'I replied, "I want an Enzo for one week."

'It went very quiet on the other end of the phone and then eventually the Ferrari man said, "OK, I have to ask my superiors about this, I don't know if this is possible."

'The next day they called back and said, "OK, we can do that, we can get you an Enzo, but we will also need one engineer from your side, a transmission engineer, who will be able to modify the shift properties and the shift speed in that transmission, together with the Golf, for one week. Vice versa. OK?"

'"OK, deal."

'So we did that. Two weeks later the Enzo arrived. It was [Ferrari Chairman] Mr di Montezemolo's personal Enzo.

'You asked me if there an exact moment when I felt that the Veyron was a very special car. It came with that Enzo. I took the Enzo out and Bugatti's president, Dr Paefgen, followed me in a Veyron. We drove out to the Autobahn and tested the cars together, swapping over and seeing what both vehicles could do. And for me, even though our car was still deep in development, I could see that the Veyron was already better than the Enzo which was a production car. And the Enzo is a brilliant car, superb. But the Veyron was better. *That* was a moment.'

If I had engineered the Veyron I would be the smuggest man in the world. I asked Dr Schreiber if the gearbox was the part of the Veyron of which he was most proud; his answer surprised me: 'No, not really. I am very proud of the DSG from our time at VW, that is really an achievement for normal public cars. For the Veyron I would say it is the combination of everything, I am proud of reaching these different targets and bringing them together in one car with a special feeling . . . it was the combination of all the challenges that was really difficult. It is relatively easy to just produce a car with 1000bhp and make it fast on a race track. It is also easy to just make a very comfortable car, but to do both in one car and one shape is much more complicated. That is what I am most proud of.'

So I asked Dr Schreiber if he is proud when he sees a Veyron: 'When I see the car I feel . . . not so much pride . . . it is more *satisfaction*. I was part of that car, I was a member of the team that managed that together. A little part of that car is *my* car. That gives me satisfaction. The Bugatti Veyron was the first car which I had the opportunity to create – within a team – the whole car. A complete car.

'The Veyron has a soul. I think that is absolutely necessary that a car like this is not just a piece of metal. Every part is well made and so on, but when the customer enters the car, he must *feel special*, he must sense a special connection. The tricky challenge is that with a team of many people working on the car and all putting their heart and soul into it, the customer must not feel overcrowded by personalities. That special connection must be written by one voice, not just the assembly of thousands of parts. One soul. One character. The Veyron.'

Now I had heard about the tumultuous development of the Veyron, the highs and lows and how Dr Schreiber, as chief engineer, had approached succeeding with this massive task, I wanted to know a little more about the man himself. It's so easy with a car like the Veyron to get wrapped up in the statistics, the numbers, but as I have said before, the more I travelled on my quest, the more I realised this was as much about *people* as it was about cars.

'Dr Schreiber, tell me, what car posters did you have on your wall as a little boy?'

'Mainly old cars, a few Bugattis but not their small cars, more of the huge vehicles like the Royale, but also many other cars, for example some Fords and later the Porsche 911 when I was a teenager. And of course the Jaguar E Type. That *shape . . .*'

'So presumably this was your dream job?'

'No, not at all. I wanted to be a lumberjack. When I was young teenager I had the dream to go to Canada and be a lumberjack. Because my parents lived in a very rural area surrounded by forests and countryside, so that was my dream, to go to Canada, to see all these trees and work with them.'

'So how did you come to be fascinated by cars?'

'Very close to our house there was a small factory where my father worked as a security guard. So when the workers had gone home, that factory was mine! It was a very old plant and one evening when I was wandering around there I found an old motorcycle in the basement. Within two weeks, with the help of my father, we had brought it back to life. I was twelve. Not long after that I banished my father from the garage and that was now my place! I would work on all these old motorbikes and I'd drive them through the forests, it was the perfect environment for learning. My father taught me a lot and by the time I was fifteen I'd begun to tune engines. That is the root of my passion for engines, for cars.

'My first "unofficial" car was a VW Beetle. I was only sixteen, and together with an older friend we spent 50 Deutschmarks and bought our own car. Although we weren't old enough, we drove that car through the local forests for more than a year. My first legal car was a Ford Capri. The older shape, the more female one.

'After school I [was an engineer's apprentice] for nearly three years and that helped me to understand things, because I made the parts by myself, I drilled them, I created all these parts of the process by myself, that was my profession. I am a man who needs the parts *in my hands*. Engineers need drawings of course, but it's better to touch parts, see the parts, understand why you have problems, only then you can *really* learn. That's my way.'

And that, it seems, is also the way of the Veyron.

After Dr Schreiber and I had finished chatting upstairs, we headed back out into the car park to wait for his ride home. I stood in the parking compound of the Bugatti workshop and research facility with night falling; the light was failing and Dr Schreiber was needing to get off.

'Mr Roach, I hope you have enjoyed the car and talking about the Veyron. Would you mind if I left you with my colleague, Frau Labersweiler?' He stretched his hand out for one final warm handshake and I thanked him for his generosity and expertise, before adding in all sincerity, 'Dr Schreiber, now I *know* there is a Santa Claus.'

Dr Schreiber jumped in a VW pick-up called an Amarok – a car he'd proudly told me was his 'new baby' and about which he spoke with the same fire in his eyes – *almost* – as when he spoke of the Veyron. He waved goodbye then accelerated quickly out of the compound, leaving me to chat to his colleague, the delightful Frau Labersweiler. I assumed we'd jump in a Golf and head back to the hotel. *This is not Bugatti.* So I was only half-surprised when she climbed in to the Super Sport and fired it up with a hearty push of her right foot. 'So, Holiday Inn, yes?'

Chatting about my day and where I lived in England, Frau Labersweiler bombed the Veyron along the main road at a fair old rate of knots, before swiftly turning into the Holiday Inn to drop me off. Along the way she'd proudly told me she has a seventeen-year-old son who's just learned to drive and has (predictably) been pestering her to get him in the Veyron. I suspect the insurance might be a tad top heavy. 'You must be some kind of Supermum, then?' I suggested, my mind boggling at the thought of what she was driving as we spoke. 'Well, I don't know about that but he seems to think it's pretty cool.' Supermum dropped me off at the hotel and I climbed out for one last round of photographs with the Super Sport. Then, with a sentimental tap of the Bugatti badge on the front grille, I turned my back on the Veyron and walked towards the hotel reception door, that beautiful engine note soundtracking my reluctant trudge back to reality. I turned and waved to Supermum . . . and then it was gone, that gleaming Bugatti Veyron Super Sport, clutching the road as if it was about to start eating the tarmac.

'I'M NOT SAYING MY VEYRON IS THE BEST EDITION, BUT IT'S IN THE TOP 1'

My first car was a Marina van. It cost more to insure than to buy, although not to me because it was my seventeenth birthday present. I traded that in for the previously mentioned bottle green Marina estate (sticking with the same dealership), a straight swap.

However, it wasn't until two years later that I paid for my very own first car, a Ford Escort. The rite of passage was complete, using money I'd saved from working at a nut-packing factory in my holidays where the foreman had one eye and I was the only person without a criminal record. Life in the fast lane, Dudley-style, as it were.

I bought my prized automobile from a car supermarket in the West Midlands. Car supermarkets were all the rage, a brand-new way to buy a car. It seemed inconceivable to just go to some apparently disused airfield (I think it was called Oldbury), look at 300 cars, all shiny and seductive and hand over some money then drive away in a spanking new car. Well, not exactly spanking, nor indeed new, but as far as I was concerned, it might as well have been. And I paid by debit card which seemed just absurd. And to this day, several years and many cars later, that first quivering car purchase witnessed the finest second-hand car dealer's spiel I've ever heard (and let's face it, we've all heard plenty). It was a blue entry-level Escort, a radio was standard but apart from that it just had seats and a steering wheel. However, it was called the 'Acapulco' *Limited Edition*. This made me feel very swanky, upwardly socially mobile, a nineteen-year-old super-achiever . . . rich, even.

But I wasn't about to have the automotive wool pulled over my eyes. I wanted to know exactly what I was getting for my money.

'It says here this is an Acapulco limited edition,' I asked, not unreasonably, in my best 'I'm-not-really-a-spotty-teenage-student-whose-never-done-this-before-and-doesn't-know-the arse-end-of-a-car-from-its-nose' voice.

'That's right, Mr Roach,' came the smooth-as-silk-and-not-at-all-patronising reply from the suited salesman, whose gelled hair would have provided ample oil should the Escort ever run dry. 'It's absolutely a limited edition vehic-ule.'

'And what exactly is limited about it?'

He pointed at the side door panel.

'The Acapulco sticker.'

I bought the car.

The Bugatti Veyron is, by definition, a limited edition. The original promise to customers was that no more than 300 coupes would be built and Bugatti have stuck to exactly that. However, there is a fascinating array of other 'limited editions' within that bulk of 300 cars as well as an additional 150 convertibles; like many celebrities, the Veyron is the master of reinvention.

The standard car was the original celebrity that stunned the world. Its own performance and technical data were uniquely bewildering and I'd seen through talking to Dr Schreiber how that celebrity came to be created. However, by stark contrast to the complexity of the engineering, on its launch there were only five colours available, all in the historically relevant two-tones associated with Bugatti. The bonnet, roof and rear of the car were painted in the darker of the two colours, with the sides and front wheel arches in the lighter shade. The list of optional extras at the point of launch was minimal too. That would soon change.

In 2008, Bugatti launched the convertible version of the world's fastest car, called the Grand Sport. The event was suitably prestigious, at Pebble Beach Concours d'Elegance in August, with production commencing in 2009. It's notable that the Veyron's celebrity had increased so much by the time of the convertible's launch that when the first ever Grand Sport was auctioned (even thought it had not yet been built), it raised $900,000 over its usual selling price for charity. The buyer would also have to have paid 10 per cent auctioneer's commission on top.

I'd seen a Grand Sport that summer's day in London with the top off, but what struck me about the car I saw at Dr Schreiber's workshop compound car park was how coherent it looks with the roof on. So many convertibles just look plain ugly with a roof up, as if it is a cumbersome afterthought. Not so the Grand Sport. Equally, Bugatti ensured that the performance was not compromised either, which is not often the case with open-top versions of certain cars.

There were a number of changes made to the Grand Sport to accommodate

Notably, the Grand Sport's doors are now made of carbon fibre instead of aluminium (as in the coupe), with further carbon-fibre struts inside to reinforce the cabin still more.

The power of the Veyron's W16 engine is a primeval noise in an open-top Grand Sport. One customer told me, 'It sounds like a jet fighter . . . you can hear it breathe.'

The Grand Sport was designed by Achim Anscheidt who would also be responsible for the Super Sport; the 'Grand Sport' name had previously been used for, among others, the Type 40 and Type 43.

BUGATTI VEYRON – A QUEST FOR PERFECTION

driving without a roof, some for speed reasons and others for safety. There were small changes to the windshield and daytime running lights. The roof itself was transparent polycarbonate; however, the core issue with any convertible car is overall weakness due to the roof being removed. In design terms, the so-called 'load paths' have to be redesigned to accommodate this and the potential extra vulnerability from side impacts and of course roll-overs. So the increased demands on the car's crash strength were reflected in an extra layer of carbon fibre and multiple reinforcement points.

The A-pillars are thicker and even the transmission tunnel is fully boxed for more strength. Cleverly, the striking 'pod' air intakes from the standard car were now reinforced to act as rollover bars, sparing the beautiful lines any rather ugly breakage in the top curves of the design. Oh, and the windows automatically locked at 93mph, presumably to save some pampered pooch's tongue.

There was no room for the removed 36lb roof in the small luggage compartment (which is only 80cm wide, 36cm long and 15cm deep!), so Bugatti came up with an admittedly rather odd-looking compromise. It was a second and more portable roof, which in essence was a large umbrella. Many critics mocked the arrangement but with so many of these cars being sold to territories such as California, it's likely that most Grand Sports will rarely have either roof in place.

The full extent of the changes was easily visible when Bugatti exhibited a cutaway of the car at the 2010 Geneva Motor Show. All the alterations meant that *with the roof down* you could still reach 229mph. With the 'umbrella' roof in place, this was limited to just 81mph. The car cost €1.4 million and the first fifty were reserved for existing 16.4 owners.

The most expensive umbrella in the world?

It wasn't long before Bugatti then announced further limited editions of this limited edition of a limited edition. The Grand Sport as we have seen was restricted to just 150 cars but Bugatti were about to get far more exclusive with a series of Grand Sports that were produced in response to customers' unique requests. The Grand Sport Sang Bleu (meaning 'blue blood') was released to mark Bugatti's centenary and was constructed from blue carbon fibre with exposed polished aluminium, with airscoops and rims highlighted in a midnight blue and a diamond-cut finish. Then there was the Grand Sport Grey Carbon which also boasted exposed carbon fibre with metallic grey, with the lower part of the bodywork showing naked polished aluminium. Further Grand Sport one-offs followed, including the Blanc Noir.

Bugatti also had a seemingly ever-expanding array of coupe special editions up their sleeve. First up had been the Pur Sang, the launch car for Bugatti's 'individualisation programme', which in stark contrast to the 16.4's very limited launch options had been designed to offer the customer a greater level of exclusivity, with an almost endless choice of optional extras.

Named in honour of Ettore Bugatti's beloved race thoroughbreds, the most notable difference between the Pur Sang and the standard two-tone Veyron was the absence of any conventional paint scheme at all – the car was still 'two-tone' but instead used bare aluminium and naked carbon fibre to fully expose the workings of the car including the passenger cabin and numerous mechanical parts. Bugatti said the Pur Sang continued the legacy of the classic Bugatti sports cars such as the Atalante, the Type 55, the Type 41 Royale. You'd need €1.4 million to buy one of only five cars produced. All of them sold instantly.

An intriguing tie-up with luxury clothing firm Hermès followed next, designed as a flagship for their respective niche expertise: the rather oddly named 'Bugatti Veyron Fbg par Hermès'. Hermès is a Paris-based saddle and leather-goods specialist, so the car was revealed in a less than appealing black-and-tan colour scheme. The interior was customised for this edition with numerous fine details and even the petrol cap was etched with the partnership. There was a slight modification of the front shape of the car too. Interestingly, the colour of the hood extended to the interior of the cockpit and re-emerged behind at the level of the rear wing. The run of this edition was just fifteen cars.

Although many observers criticised the black-and-tan colour scheme as unflattering, the real fascination with the Hermès was the history behind it. The respective company founders, Emile Hermès and Ettore Bugatti, had become friends in the 1920s after the latter had ordered a bespoke suitcase for his first Bugatti Royale (modern-day Hermès bags can sell for upwards of $100,000). The car's rather awkward name refers to the headquarters on the Rue du Faubourg

On the Veyron Fbg par Hermès the front grille carries the company monogram, the roadwheels have a single H in the centre, and the fuel-filler door is engraved with Bugatti Veyron Fbg par Hermès.

The interior is fitted in Hermès leather with internal door handles reminiscent of handles used on Hermès trunks – a Hermès wallet and Hermès suitcase is included.

Following criticism of the paint scheme, the Hermès was later offered in four new colour schemes: 'Indigo Blue and Vermilion', 'Indigo Blue and Lime Green', 'Black and Garance Red', and 'Prussian Blue and Blue Jean'.

The air vents around the edges mimic Hermès' saddle-stitching. Inside, the usual brushed aluminium dash is replaced with hand-processed calfskin leather.

The horseshoe radiator grille and the lateral ventilation grilles flanking it are made from lightweight alloys with a design of interlocking H's evoking the Hermès 'signature'.

Saint-Honoré (the Fbg being short for Faubourg), where Hermès created custom interiors for some of Bugatti's cars during the 1920s. Bugatti press released the car as a perfect collaboration between a 'car-loving saddle-maker' and a 'horse-loving car-maker'.

An ultra-rare Veyron – i.e. there's one – was unveiled at the 2009 Geneva Motor Show, the so-called Bleu Centenaire, produced to celebrate the brand's centenary. The entire body was painted in a combination of matte and gloss 'Bugatti sprint-blue', it had a light-cream interior and the (first) painted engine cover.

Then came the Sang Noir, the darker brother of the Pur Sang. Said to be inspired by the legendary Bugatti Type 57S Atlantic, the Sang Noir features unpainted carbon-fibre sections but in this car the aluminium sections are painted black, giving the car a very dark, almost ominous effect. The interior is kitted out in natural leather akin to that of the Atlantic. Fifteen cars were made, with most selling in the United States.

Perhaps not surprisingly, the Middle East has been a profitable market for the Veyron. To mark this, Bugatti produced a limited edition of three individual cars specially designed for that territory: the Nocturne, the Sang d'Argent, and a Grand Sport called Soliel de Nuit.

Bugatti also released four special-edition cars at the Concorso d'Eleganza in the Villa d'Este in Como as part of their centenary celebrations. The so-called 'Bugatti Veyron Type 35 Grand Prix Homage' cars were made in honour of the Type 35 Grand Prix car and the racers who drove them, namely Jean-Pierre Wimille, Achille Varzi, Malcolm Campbell and Hermann zu Leiningen.

The five-car production Nocturne has galvanised side windows to blend in with the polished aluminium body panel accents; polished custom wheels and a black 'nanocoated magnesium dashboard' with a centre console rendered in galvanised platinum. The hood is covered in polished aluminium which serves to elongate the look of this Bug.

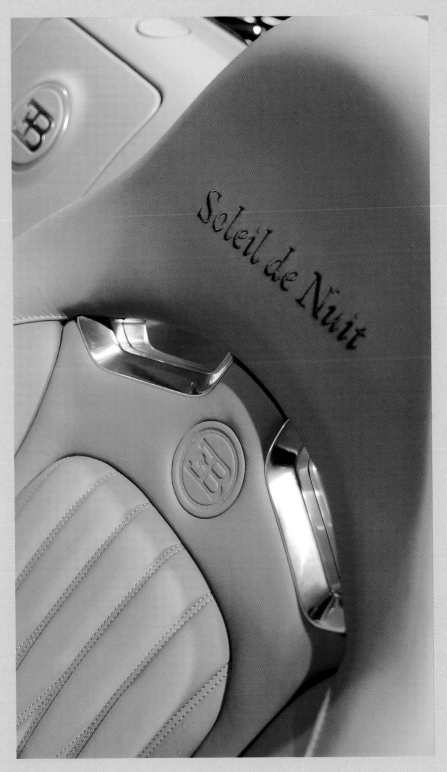

The Soleil de Nuit Grand Sport has a silver metallic lower portion of the bodywork and an impressively deep blue finish on the upper, complemented by a 'burnt orange' interior with quilted seats.

The Sang d'Argent has a silver-themed finish with polished aluminium on the doors and front wings; its alloy wheels are taken from the Grand Sport design. The car is a one-off.

The 'Jean-Pierre Wimille' is bright blue, the 'Achille Varzi' is crimson red, the 'Malcolm Campbell' is dark green and the 'Hermann zu Leiningen' is off-white. The cars feature chrome front fenders and doors.

With many of these limited editions, Bugatti quoted their historical brand ethic, 'Art-Forme-Technique', which summed up Ettore's approach to car design and manufacture. However, many observers criticised the amount of limited editions with many less than positive reports being published in several magazines.

The exclusivity of the Veyron has now reached such heights that customers can effectively create their own 'edition' Veyron, so vast is the bewildering array of optional extras and personal touches that can be added. Recently, one car was even gilded in gold plate. Outside of official Bugatti circles, there is also a market where other firms customise the car, such as the tuning house Mansory who produced the 'Linea Vincero', a one-off Veyron which included a fully modified aero-kit, LED lighting, new wheels and highly polished carbon-fibre body panels that include copper threads interwoven into the surface. Most notably perhaps was their tuning upgrade – previous limited-edition Veyrons did not boast higher performance stats – with Mansory achieving a power upgrade to 1109bhp and 967ft/lb torque, via an upgraded cooling system and exhaust set-up. In total, these modifications added nearly $1 million to the Veyron base price.

Perhaps the most striking fact about these various beautiful limited editions and one-off Veyrons is that as a result – as with my Ford Escort 1.4L Acapulco – the 16.4 standard car is now effectively an 'entry level' model.

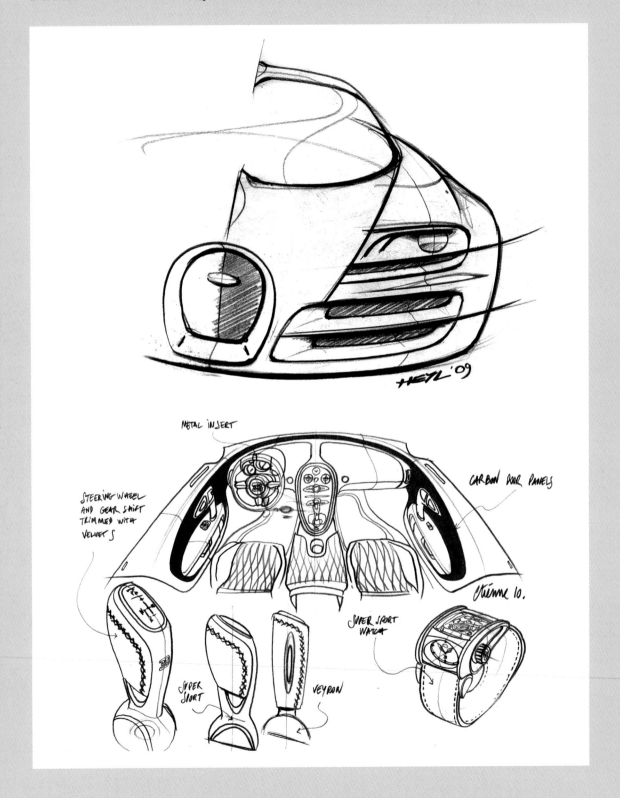

THE BUGATTI VEYRON SUPER SPORT

For me, if I had to own one Veyron from all the various editions on offer, it would be 'my' Super Sport. The fastest road car of all time. On the day I'd been lucky enough to drive one, I told Dr Schreiber that I presumed this brutally extreme version of the car had been a response to the American SS Aero trumping the Bugatti's top speed of 253mph. 'Not so,' he said. 'It was a reaction to numerous customer requests saying, "My Veyron is a really good car but I'd like it more aggressive, both in look and in driving." Some customers just wanted more power.'

'Of course, because 1001bhp isn't enough . . .' I joked.

'They just wanted more power. So we decided to evaluate the technical requirements to increase the horses from the standard car. First of all we looked at the engine and found that the basis of that should be able to produce 1200 horses. But we needed more boost pressure, we needed 10 per cent bigger turbochargers, bigger openings at the front for better air flow, we needed bigger intercoolers and we also found that we had to do some reinforcements for the whole drive train, the transmission too; some gears were weak as the additional power had generated another 250Nm of torque, up to 1500Nm, which is pretty massive. And we had to modify the gear ratio for the seventh gear because of the higher top speed; we also had to reinforce the rear axle, reinforce the drive shafts, more or less the complete drive train.

'But this was not so hard to do as develop the original car. To reach the goals for the Super Sport – 1200 horses, 1500Nm of torque and a higher top speed – was easier because the team was convinced from the beginning that we would reach these goals, plus we were much better skilled, they were effectively already trained.'

You may well ask why it takes an extra 200bhp to add only 14mph to the top speed of the standard Veyron. That's because the resistance of the wind at such speeds is not linear, it actually increases by the cube of the speed. In layman's terms, this means that the increase in resistance is not gradual, it's like hitting a brick wall. Hence to increase the Super Sport's speed by 1km/h required a full 8bhp to be added.

BUGATTI VEYRON – A QUEST FOR PERFECTION

'The fact that the Super Sport exists in the first place is, we feel, reason in itself to celebrate. It is, after all, the ultimate creation on four wheels – the point at which whatever progress has been made by the motor car over the past century can be measured, at its most extreme, its most expensive and, yes, its excessive best.' *Autocar's* 5000th road test, 2 March 2011.

Weight was again an issue, with the Super Sport being stripped of over 110lb from the basic model; the new, stiffer carbon-fibre weave in the cabin saved 55lb alone. The unique wheels shaved a further 25lb off the waist. This helped Bugatti actually increase fuel consumption by 10 per cent.

Visually the Super Sport is much sleeker, with the impressive coolers from the standard car removed and replaced with flush-fitted NACA ducts (an air inlet 'scoop' originally pioneered in the aerospace industry) in the roof. Extra cooling ducts were also fitted beneath the headlights. To me, it looks like a bullet, which is pretty much what it is in automotive terms.

To take the world's most extreme and expensive car and then 'pimp' it up to devastatingly fast proportions – and costs – must have raised a few eyebrows in the Bugatti accounts department. So I'd asked Dr Schreiber if

there was a moment when the engineers' ambition had to be reined in due to cost.

'A few times, yes,' he'd replied with a wry smile. 'When you stand behind the Super Sport you see these huge newly designed exhaust pipes. Around these pipes you have a thin cover to prevent damage to the carbon fibre parts and this cover is made out of steel. Originally some of my guys said they wanted to make it out of ceramic because of the better heat protection properties, others were of the opinion that we should use titanium which is very light and becomes blue when it's hot, so the customer could see how hot his exhaust system was! The ceramic was ten times the price; even the titanium was about three times the cost, so we decided that this was just too much, it was not necessary, the steel protection is still superb.'

The standard Veyron engine was found in tests to actually be producing on average around 1050bhp but Bugatti left the figure at 1001bhp because that is what Dr Piëch had promised. So the increase to 1200bhp for the Super Sport was a task that Dr Schreiber was entirely confident of achieving.

The roof was extended rearward and largely obscures the engine, a double diffuser was fitted in the rear and a redesigned exhaust pipe was also added.

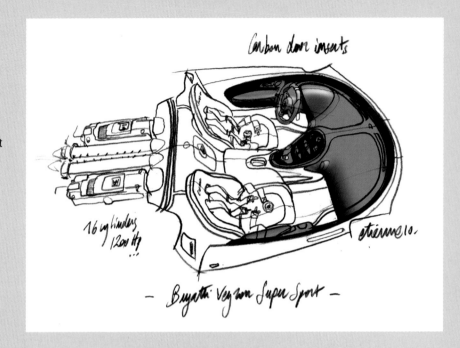

Bugatti invested heavily in the Super Sport with a massive number of brand-new designs and parts created for the project. They calculated that they needed to sell twenty-five cars to make it a profitable exercise; at the time of writing they have sold almost 50 per cent more than this target. The Super Sport tapped neatly into Bugatti's tradition of building super sport versions of successful models, most notably the Type 57S. And the performance? That bizarre 1200bhp generated the same 0–60 as the 16.4 (2.5 seconds), but then afterwards the stats were sizeably more striking. There was that gargantuan 1106ft/lb, or 1500Nm, of torque and a top speed limited to 258mph 'to protect the tyres'. The public debut was at the Pebble Beach Concours d'Elegance in August 2010, and despite the hefty price tag, there were more takers than cars for the first production run.

However, it wasn't the price that the Super Sport became famous for; instead it was the 2010 world record as the fastest road production car ever. The man in the driving seat that day was Bugatti test driver Pierre-Henri Raphanel. His email signature is the perfectly fantastic 'Pilote Officiel', which seemed entirely apt given the speed he travelled that day.

Pierre had enjoyed a long and fruitful seventeen-year career as a racing driver years before he worked with Bugatti. This included Formula Renault, Formula 3, Formula 3000 and even Formula 1 drives. After that he worked for Toyota and McLaren in endurance races and also competed at Le Mans fourteen times, coming in the top three multiple times and even winning the GT category for McLaren.

The speed and angle of deployment of the rear wing/air brake was completely recalibrated for the Super Sport – otherwise, the car would have been 'terminally unstable'. The bi-plane wing now deploys at 180kph and at a different speed/angle to the standard car (220kph). At top speed this generates 882lb of downforce.

He'd actually retired and involved himself in real estate when he received a call from Bugatti's Thomas Bscher asking if he'd like to join four other drivers presenting the new Bugatti to VW group members and potential customers in the autumn of 2005. At this point, Pierre-Henri openly admits he knew nothing about the car: 'I had no idea about the Veyron, I had been out of motoring altogether for some time. I thought the name Veyron was to do with the two-colour combinations, I thought it was because of the French for 'les yeux vairons' which means one eye is in one colour and one eye in another. Then I found out about Pierre Veyron! So I was a Bugatti virgin!'

And what was his reaction when he drove the car for the very first time? 'It was a shock, a real shock. I stayed in the car for seven hours, I did not want to leave the car because if I did someone else would get in my place, so I ate my lunch in there, I had my drinks in there, I never got out. It is so different to anything you could expect, from anything I had been racing even, and I have experience of fast cars obviously – in Japan I'd driven a racer with 1200bhp, so I knew all about high speeds but this was a tremendous amount of power mixed with civility too.

'We had no time before the event to get introduced to the car so when I then stepped out with the first potential customer, I was discovering the speed and power at the same time as them, I was sharing their experience. I was so excited, it was such a discovery. The first time I put my foot down it was a massive shock. It is something unreal, it's such huge power and acceleration yet it's not on a race track, it's in a normal, everyday environment. Racing drivers operate in a different world, there is a degree of security driving in a racing environment, but the Bugatti lets you do this on normal roads. It's like activating what I call an "adrenaline box machine".'

The Super Sport's vital statistics: 1106ft/lb; top speed of 258mph – limited to protect the tyres; 0–62mph in 2.5sec; 0–124mph in 6.7sec; 0–186mph in 14.6sec; standing quarter mile in 9.7sec and a mile in 23.6sec.

Dr Schreiber receiving a plaque to certify the world record speed for a production car, achieved by the Super Sport. In the background wearing the hat is Bugatti's then-President Dr Paefgen.

The top-secret Ehra-Lessien test track is used by VW for high-speed testing. It contains sixteen miles of private road, a high speed oval and a straight of more than five miles long.

It remains the most shocking experience of power for Pierre: 'I'd been emotional when I first drove the F1 for McLaren, and driving a pure racing car for Le Mans was amazing too, but to drive the Veyron on the road was very emotional. It had such pure performance delivery, I'd experienced this kind of performance on a track before, but I'd never thought this could be possible on a road. If you floor it in a Super Sport, your neck will feel broken. I frequently come back from customer days and have neck problems. The power is *massive*.'

Some 3500 Veyron test drives later, Bugatti decided to see if the Super Sport could break the speed record for a production car. 'It had not been the number one priority for Bugatti to achieve the world record,' continues Pierre. 'The Super Sport was created to meet the customer's wishes for a more extreme Veyron. There is a big difference.

'When there was a chance to go for the world record, I said I wanted to be the man in the car for that. I'd done 400km/h+ many, many times previously. The day of the record was a very, very stressful time. They did all the tests to prepare the car at the high speed level. I arrived at Ehra-Lessien three days earlier and drove many preparation runs. Previously I'd driven close to the guard rail, but I discovered that in this area of extremely high speed, namely faster than 425km/h, the car was better towards the centre lane. The tarmac there is very good but it's not made for 425+. I found the smallest imperfection was making a big interaction in the car so I decided to stay in the centre lane.

'On some of the test runs at the very top speeds I was feeling vibrations in the car, but the engineers could not find a problem. Then we realised it was the tarmac. It's like shaving – the tarmac had a grain in it when travelling the opposite

way, and this created micro-vibrations at 430+km/h which really impacted on the stability of the car. This was highly stressful. There were unknown areas.'

It was actually forbidden to run at high speed in the opposite direction so Pierre had to sign a waiver accepting responsibility and the risk. 'Signing that waiver in itself created pressure. People were telling me that nothing was going to go wrong, but the waiver form made me feel that it might.

'The night before the record attempt I kept waking up as I had so much adrenaline in my veins having done all the test runs, including eight at speeds over 425km/h. At one point I woke up at 4.27 a.m. and I thought, *That will be my top speed*, but then I woke up again and it was 4.40! *Oh no!* So I went back to sleep.'

Speaking to Pierre you get a real sense of the risk, regardless of the technology, the safety measures, the analysis, the driving expertise; this was still two tons of car travelling at nearly a third of the speed of sound. On the actual morning of the attempt, he was surprised to find that the tyres were the ones he'd used the day before.

'The margins were very tight. I spoke to the engineer in the morning and he told me they'd run a bench test on the tyres in the factory at 435km/h. I said, "And how long did the tyres last?" And he said, "No more than four minutes." Then I noticed the tyres on the Veyron were the same ones I'd been using the day before! I asked him if I was getting a new set of tyres and he said, "No need, we are still in that four minute window, it will be OK." I could only hope that he was correct.

'I felt I had a chance to die that day. That is not a nice feeling. When I sat in the car about to go, I felt that potentially fatal risk. It was stressful. I think it was a very stressful day for everyone on the team too, because if something went wrong they would have had to live with that for the rest of their lives. So it was very emotional. For me, it was a mental exercise. The physical corrections I had to make in the car were very slight, it was much more mental. It was an undeniable fact that if something happened, I would not come back to the pit. It was scary . . . and exciting too, if I am honest.'

The first run was exactly 427km/h (actually 427.9km/h, some 265.9mph), just as Pierre-Henri had seen on his clock. The required return leg was the most demanding – he knew that the crash barriers were not constructed to withstand impact from that direction and as he hit the 425 mark, the car began to vibrate against the grain of the tarmac again, but he went even faster and ran 434.2km/h (269.8mph).

The stresses on the car at this speed are immense. Even the dirt on the bonnet causes drag. Pierre-Henri feels that the speeds past 425 were the most risky: 'At that speed, 120+ metres per second, you cannot interfere with the car,

you cannot do anything, if you try to interfere it will be a huge disaster, you are more a passenger than a driver, you have to try to be as small as possible in the car, let the car do what the car wants to do, when it wants to do it. This feeling is not usual for a race driver. Up to say 425 the car is as solid as a rock. After that it is not as comfortable, there starts to be interference, not from the car but from the tarmac.'

And yet the 'pilot' will not take the lion's share of credit, heralding instead the team effort on the day. 'I felt I brought an extra one, maybe two km/h. That was my decision. On the reverse run I postponed the braking point because I felt if I could continue a little further I could run in the forest more and be shielded from the wind for longer, so the speed could be faster. I'd decided this the day before and that's what I did, which maybe gained one or two kilometres. That was my contribution.'

And if the car was rerun on a perfect track on an ideal day with 100 per cent perfect conditions, could the Super Sport go even faster? 'There would not be much more speed to be had. We were very close to the edge. We didn't know what would happen next. Would one more kilometre of speed be acceptable or would the car – and me – disappear in a second? It was *that close* to the edge.'

Pierre-Henri also holds the record for a Bugatti at the Prescott Speed Hill Climb, set in Gotherington, Gloucestershire (home to the Bugatti Trust and the Bugatti Owner's Club). He broke the long-standing Type 51's record. Pierre-Henri is pictured here with Dr Schreiber.

The record attempt was televised as part of an episode in Series 9 of *Top Gear*. As we have noted, the team sent James May, or Captain Slow as he is nicknamed, to attempt to break the record (Bugatti are rumoured to have a little book of the customers that they can confirm have also achieved such a speed). 'What I found weird about it, and this will seem absurd,' May later revealed in the *Daily Mail*, 'is that 253mph feels a lot faster than 200mph. At 250, it suddenly gets to the point where things are happening faster than you can process the information.'

It's worth a quick aside to just explain what the world looks like at 267mph in a Super Sport and therefore what this 'celebrity' car is actually capable of in pure automotive terms. Dr Kerry Spackman, the eminent neuroscientist and motorsport expert who'd helped me contact VW as part of my quest, knows the science behind driving at such prodigious speeds: 'It's not just the sheer speed, it's the visual richness coming by. So if you're in a jumbo jet doing 500mph, and you're looking out of the window at this great big fluffy cloud in the distance going by, it's no big deal because it's not visually rich, the clouds are big and they go past at a distance.

'However, when you're close to the ground and certain things are going by at a very high speed, your brain gets overloaded. What tends to happen then is you get tunnel vision where everything outside a certain area isn't processed, you can see it but your brain just decides there's just too much going on out there, all it can really focus on is what's immediately in front of it in a small area. So you can see everything but you can't do anything with that vision, the brain says it's all too complicated to deal with.

'If you think about it, the human brain evolved over millions of years to deal with a top speed of about 30km/h if you're lucky on a horse, or less if you are running. If you tune something for the normal environment it operates in, it works very well. Even up to about 50km/h, we are pretty aware of everything around us; however, as you get faster and faster, you start to attend to less and less.

'What's happening in a Veyron at 267 is that at some point the brain just simply can't cope with everything, so instead of trying to resolve all the detail, your brain starts to take short cuts. And it's a non-linear process. So 300km/h isn't just three times 100km/h. There's a real transition where it suddenly gets hard.' That a motorsport neuroscientist can talk about the brain function in such a way gives you some idea of just how other-worldly the car is. There's fast and there's *Bugatti Veyron fast*.

To mark the record-beating occasion, the first five Super Sports sold were called 'World Record Editions' (costing £1,950,000), bedecked in that striking black-and-orange livery which had greeted me that day outside the Holiday Inn. They come complete with an extra set of tyres, as well as a racing suit and helmet.

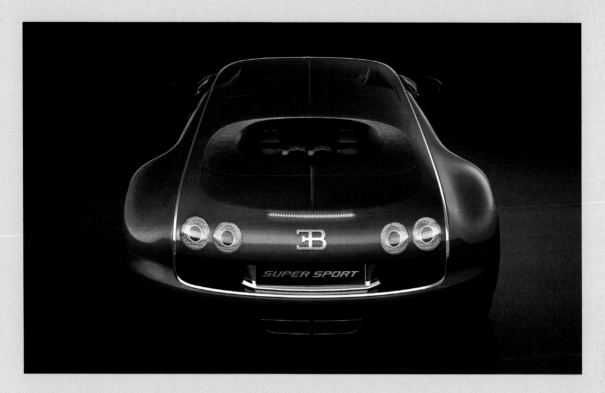

Of course, there are rival cars out there that seem determined to snatch the mantle of 'fastest car ever' back from Bugatti. Perhaps the strongest challenger is the Shelby SSC Ultimate Aero, made by a company whose founder invented a revolutionary scanning system for breast cancer. The car reaches 256mph but his marque is said to be in development for a new generation of Aero that has a reported top speed potential of over 300mph and over 1350bhp, in a vehicle that weighs just over a third as much as a Veyron. Elsewhere, the Transtar Dagger GT comes with an estimated top speed of 314mph.

But can you drive them to the opera?

CHAPTER TWELVE

THE ARTIST'S WORKSHOP

My quest had already taken me to Wolfsburg, I'd driven the mythical beast and met the chief engineer behind this celebrity's bewildering performance. I'd soaked in the Autostadt to get a flavour of the corporate culture that had attempted this feat, yet come away from there with memories of *people* as well as speed. But I wanted to know more. I now knew how the Veyron had come about, how it had been developed and its celebrity life to date; what I wanted to know – as with any celebrity I work with – was what goes into their day-to-day life to keep that celebrity aflame? In this case, how was the car itself made? Where? And by whom?

So I set off on the road once more, this time heading to Molsheim where the Veyron factory itself is located, in the Alsace region of eastern France. Before I arrived at this Bugatti mecca, I had arranged to meet the brand's historian, Julius Kruta, at the Cité de l'Automobile in Mulhouse, some fifty-five miles from Molsheim. This huge building houses the so-called 'Schlumpf' museum, the biggest car collection in the world with over 400 vehicles on show, so vast that there is even a small indoor train to carry visitors around; most poignantly for my book, the museum boasts the world's largest collection of rare and vintage Bugattis, so ahead of my trip to Molsheim it seemed like a perfect opportunity to soak up the history.

Set in an old textile factory – the Schlumpf family had made their money in that industry – the building is an imposing sight, festooned at the entrance with oversized model cars hanging from towering wire sculptures. These matched the lofty ambitions of the Schlumpf brothers who had set out to buy every Bugatti in the world when they first started their collection in the 1950s (they acquired 130, not quite every one).

Julius was perfectly on time and arrived with a group of Japanese motor journalists. They would be my companions for the tour of the museum, all chatting away and snapping photographs constantly. Julius was wearing a Bugatti coat and looked much younger than I'd expected for such a revered brand historian – prior to our meeting one source had described him as like 'a friendly walking encyclopaedia'. Within minutes of talking to him, it was clear that not only was he a Bugatti super-expert, he was most obviously a *car person*.

He took us around the museum and painstakingly and patiently explained minute details of every Bugatti we came across. Julius's knowledge of Bugatti was breathtaking, his passion for the cars infectious. Listening to him talk in such detail and with that fire I had now come to recognise in all the Bugatti people I'd been meeting, I was transported back in time to when Ettore Bugatti vied with Ferdinand Porsche on a handful of race courses across Europe, when automobiles were in their very infancy and eccentrics, mavericks and unique characters shaped the future of the industry. This was a time before corporate takeovers, computers and manufacturing robots, global advertising campaigns and market shares. Innocent? Perhaps that's too idealistic a phrase, but certainly there was a purity from that period that is by definition impossible to assimilate in the modern era.

Bugatti's history is above all a story of creativity. Ettore Bugatti was an Italian born in Milan in 1881. He came from a family of artists, his father Carlo being a revered art nouveau furniture and jewellery designer famed for using exotic materials. Carlo's own father was an artistic carpenter, a trait inherited by Ettore's younger brother Rembrandt who would go on to become a noted *animalier* sculptor in his own right. Even Ettore's aunt lived with the painter Giovanni Segantini. Not surprisingly, creative thinking was at the heart of the Bugatti household and such skills as painting, or working with clay and wood, were openly taught and encouraged in the family home.

During Ettore's teenage years, the dawn of motoring was hard to ignore and he quickly became fascinated by these remarkable new machines. Perhaps it was in these formative years that a personal creative synergy between engineering and art was forged that would eventually change the face of automotive history.

His first job was as an apprentice at a local Milanese tricycle manufacturer called Prinetti & Stucchi, which was an ideal training ground for discovering elementary engineering principles. It quickly became apparent that a conventional career was never going to satiate the artistic and individualistic fire in his young belly. Ettore's first foray into creating his own vehicle came when he attached four existing engines to a tricycle; before long he'd designed his own motor car using axles he'd bought off the shelf. The construction was so remarkable that this first car design won an award at an internationally renowned industry fair in Milan.

His artistic family environment had blessed him with a creative eye that meant engineering draughtsmanship came very naturally; he sketched prolifically and over 20,000 of these drawings have survived, including designs for fishing boats, spaghetti machines and medical instruments. He would eventually own over 500 patents.

At the same time – and this was true throughout his colourful career –

technical form was never the prime mover, Ettore would always design by *instinct*. 'His first effort [at a car] was quite attractive in its whole appearance and layout,' explained Bugatti's historian Julius, 'and a factory owner from Niederbronn, Alsace called Baron de Dietrich saw this car and was interested in hiring the young engineer who had designed it. Ettore was still a minor in 1901 and so he asked his father Carlo to sign the contract.' Working for this Alsatian magnate, the young Ettore produced his very early cars, branded as De Dietrich-Bugattis.

However, Ettore's independent spirit was as fierce as his artistic streak, so after two years he was sacked, essentially because he didn't do what his boss asked of him – he was meant to design trucks and buses but instead he dreamed up race cars. He'd already personally competed in many of the road races that littered the European towns of the late nineteenth century, and his thirst for speed was considerable. 'He was very extravagant,' explained Julius, 'pictures of him back then tell us this much, you could even consider him a dandy, his hairstyle, the way he dressed was really different.'

In such formative years of the car industry, it's important to remember that there was no engineering degree course that aspiring young mechanics could attend, no formal education to teach the manufacture of a motor car. So Ettore learned his craft by working for other companies including Deutz Gasmotoren Fabrik in Cologne. He soon accumulated enough money to start his own company in Molsheim in 1909, the same year that his first son Jean was born (he'd married his wife Barbara in 1907). Manufacture of his own marque was sparked by the so-called Type 10 prototype that he'd built in his spare time in his own basement while still working for Deutz.

Why Molsheim? 'It was a pure coincidence,' explained Julius, 'because he asked his right-hand man where to find cheap grounds to start his own company. Obviously they knew Alsace quite well, back then it was a very rural place (it's more industrial now), and Molsheim was in the heart of Europe, so it made sense to Ettore.' So Bugatti took up a lease on an old dye works in Molsheim, just a few miles west of Strasbourg. For some contemporaries, this was an odd choice: 'If you think about the major luxury brands in France, they are all based around Paris, but Bugatti was in Molsheim. In those society days, you would either live in Paris or abroad, not in the French countryside, but that's not Bugatti!' Ettorre's company commenced officially on 1 January 1910; he would soon adopt the moniker of 'Le Patron' and seeing photos of him strolling around the factory's grounds in his bowler hat and pristine suit, the title seems entirely appropriate.

At this point, pre-First World War, Alsace was in Germany, so the racing cars that Ettore Bugatti created were painted white; only after the war did Alsace return to France and then his beloved racers were sent out in that distinctive blue livery.

'I say that it is in my opinion impossible to design a better machine. During the period I have been the owner of this car, I have never had any trouble.'

Letter of compliment written by Brigadier General McCoskry Butt in 1904 concerning the De Dietrich cars which Ettore Bugatti was designing in young adulthood.

Ettore Bugatti created cars that were at the cutting edge of this period, models such as the T13; he even put his skills to aeroplane engines. The war interrupted his efforts but after the conflict he returned to Molsheim and reopened his factory. His key prowess at this point was always *lightweight* cars and this manifested itself with great success in the many races around Europe.

As Julius walked us around the museum, I was most struck by the early racing pedigree of Bugatti, and it was hard not to make the comparison that today there is no such competitive branch of the brand. Some historians suggest that a young Enzo Ferrari dreamed of becoming as great as Ettore Bugatti. Many of Ettore's customers were racing drivers, particularly for vehicles such as the Type 35s, and it seemed that the air he breathed was rich with the oxygen and language of the track. Ettore sold more than 300 Type 35s, slightly more than the total number of Veyrons.

These cars were also – to quote Dr Schreiber – 'easy to use' in that you could drive to a grand prix in a Type 35, take off the mudguards and lights, go out and win the race, then drive home afterwards. With later models like the Type 50, this was taken one step further, as this was a big touring saloon that could also easily be raced to a very high standard. This was an ethos that was very dear to Ettore; there had always been a demand for road cars that possessed the attributes of racing specimens, but few manufacturers of this era were able to capture this balance with such finesse. It is a fact that all Bugatti racing cars were derivatives from touring cars. In terms of the Veyron, that's an important genealogical point.

Ettore Bugatti and Jean Bugatti

'Developing cars only for racing was not something that was in Ettore's mind,' expanded Julius. 'Something like a [Mercedes] silver arrow W125 or W154, you could never ever imagine driving these cars on the road, but even the [brutally fast] Bugatti Type 59 from 1933/34 was a car you could drive on the road.' As a consequence, with a rash of grands prix contested every week, Bugatti was hugely prolific in his racing victories, eventually scooping over 2000 race wins. Cars such as the legendary Brescia were truly dominant.

Bugatti was never a volume producer; in the thirty years of his original tenure at Molsheim, he only produced 7800 cars. That's what VW in Wolfsburg make in two days. However, by name, heritage and image, Bugatti was a huge car *brand*.

Bugatti wasn't just about innovative cars; he was also a marketing genius. 'He was an extreme marketing talent,' opined Julius, 'particularly in spending every penny he had and every penny he didn't have. He bought the 1857-built château and grounds [near to the factory] on 3 May 1928 but he didn't need that, he had no reason to have it. He regarded himself as the king of Molsheim when he bought it and he certainly was the industrial king of that town. But he never lived in the château, he lived in his villa next to the factory, he only used the château for the same reason Bugatti does today: to represent the brand, throw banquets, welcome clients, and Ettore would hold some shooting events too.' (Ettore's parents, Carlo and Teresa Bugatti, lived in one of the former coach houses in their old age.)

He'd market the brand in other clever ways too. When Ettore's son Roland was five, his father built him a half-scale Type 35 to race around the factory grounds. When wealthy customers saw this one-off toy, they pleaded with Ettore to make their children the same, and so he began a sideline in perfect miniature toy replicas – some of which can command around £70,000 in today's collector's market.

'He was a marketing genius,' Julius stated. 'He put his signature on his cylinder heads, the engines, the EB logo was everywhere, he was doing brochures where you'd find the signature and EB initials very often, he used the brand name heavily. He promoted it, he advertised in newspapers and he even had a slogan then – car companies have them today and change them every few years, but back then he said Bugatti's was, "Le pur sang des automobiles" – "The thoroughbred of cars". He promoted this phrase and Bugatti still use it today, it's perfect, there's nothing to add. He was as much a pioneer of branding as he was of cars.' Ettore was a horse lover and this choice of words was deliberate; he even kept numerous thoroughbred racehorses at his factory site.

For Julius, there are two Bugatti periods: the years of innovation and the era of design. 'The first innovative period was the years from the marque's birth until the mid-1920s, where you have a single overhead-cam 16-valve 4-cylinder engine in an extremely light car that's agile and very interesting and could be considered as a milestone.'

Such milestones attracted mavericks and super-achievers. Just as with the modern-day Veyron, many of the people that Bugatti created cars for were equally unique. Take Roland Garros, for example, the famous race driver and aviator (who would later lend his name to the French Open tennis stadium) – he asked for a car that would be as fast as his fighter plane, ideally surpassing 160km/h. Remember, this was way back in 1912. And when the customers visited Ettore at his factory, they found a workshop that was as aesthetically masterminded by Le Patron as his cars. Just as I'd seen in Dr Schreiber's workshop, in Ettore's original workshop the EB logo was everywhere, even on workbenches and tools. Ettore went further, though; he designed those workbenches, he even designed and built the vices on the workbenches. The oak doors to the factory were Bugatti originals. The handles on those doors were solid brass, beautifully shaped, and he insisted on them being polished every evening. And polished they were, with a cloth stitched with his initials. Ettore saw his factory as simply another work of art.

The detail on his cars was even more impeccable. The obvious design and visual appeal was plain to see; but beneath the body panels you would find engines held together by initialled EB bolts, his name or initials emblazoned across parts of the car that few people ever saw. And this was not just self-indulgence – Ettore knew that by designing his own screws, his customers would then need custom-made tools (bought from him of course!) to look after their charges. And like the Veyron, most of the parts for his cars were anything but 'off the shelf'.

Despite being a fairly dictatorial boss – at least in terms of design ethics and his company's vision – Ettore respected and admired his workers, so when these employees joined the strikes that ruptured France in the mid-1930s, he was devastated, appalled that his beloved workforce would betray him in such a fashion. So he moved to Paris and a less emotional bond with Molsheim sprouted where once there had been only adoration. His son Jean then 'inherited' Molsheim and began to build equally remarkable cars there, running the operation from 1936.

This brings us to the second great period of Bugatti, the design classics which are probably more widely known today – essentially Jean Bugatti's period from the mid-1920s until the end of the 1930s. Technically these cars were not ahead of the game any more, and Bugatti was not winning so many grands prix by now. There were major victories, but by the 1930s the German and Italian opposition had taken racing to another level, boosted by considerable government subsidies. The 1934 Belgian GP was the French marque's last-ever GP victory.

'When you took the bodywork off this second era of Bugatti cars,' explained Julius, 'they were not ahead of the game, but the quality of attention to detail and the level of hours put into the finish was second to none. The cars were beautiful, the Type 57s, the 55S, the Type 50, the Atlantic, they are iconic designs and looked fantastic then as they do today.'

There is a certain irony to this mantel, as Jean considered himself a manager and engineer, in contrast to the artistic flair of his father, yet it is Jean's dazzling and truly artistic designs for which Bugatti is often most admired. Like his father, this flair was also rooted in practicality, as Jean knew personally how to hammer body panels, fix footboards and even the best way to polish a finished car.

Although many cite the grandiose design legend the Royale as a 'flop' car (because it sold so few and was never owned by anyone of regal blood), in a sense this landmark car 'saved' Bugatti – because from the ashes of this vehicle he won a contract to design and build trains for the French railway network. His distinctive trains utilised two or even four engines taken from the Royale, chiefly because the enormous torque they generated was ideal for this use.

In 1939 Bugatti triumphed at Le Mans, the manufacturer's second and last victory in that famous race. But tragically, only a few weeks after the Bugatti race drivers Veyron and Wimille passed the chequered flag at Le Mans first, the famous marque had the centre of its universe wrenched out. On the evening of 11 August 1939, Jean Bugatti was testing the exact same car that had carried Veyron to Le Mans victory just a few days earlier. Two Bugatti workers stopped all traffic on the main road between Molsheim and Strasbourg to allow for a safe high-speed run. They had to light up the tachometer with a cigarette because the factory hadn't yet had a chance to fit illumination bulbs on the panel; during the first four runs, Jean's co-driver shouted out what revs-per-minute he was achieving. They drove those four laps together before Jean asked to drive the final lap alone, so his colleague could observe the car's behaviour from afar.

On that fateful last lap, a cyclist pulled out into the path of the speeding Bugatti. Jean somehow managed to avoid a collision but in doing so veered off the road at over 200km/h, hit a tree, was hurled out of the car and killed instantly in a massive crash that sliced the car in two. He was just thirty (there is now a monument at the site of the fatal accident near Duppigheim); ironically, Jean had rarely raced, as his father usually forbade him. Within two weeks, the Second World War had started and Ettore was forced to flee Molsheim in the wake of the occupying Nazi army. The Type 57 was never rebuilt. From many perspectives, not least both personal and professional, Bugatti was a broken dream.

After the Second World War, the ruling aristocracy and social elite of Europe was sorely diluted, perhaps terminally. Luxury brands faced a barren period and Bugatti was no exception. On the Continent, the upper classes had been decimated by the social upheaval after the war and with this social sea-change Ettore's core market effectively evaporated. In an attempt to survive, he designed cars such as the Type 68, smaller and more efficient yet also still luxurious but this was never built (an economy car he'd developed to rival the 2CV sadly also never materialised).

By now the Bugatti legend was peppered with tragedy. As mentioned, Ettore's brother Rembrandt was a talented sculptor who had created the only mascot Bugatti ever placed on one of its cars – the towering elephant proudly sitting on the front of the Royale. The animal was chosen by Ettore because it was 'the biggest and the greatest' of all animals. But Rembrandt committed suicide in 1916 aged only thirty-one – some historians suggest his deep despair came from the trauma he suffered when Antwerp Zoo was forced to cull most of its livestock, which he'd spent years lovingly sculpting, during the First World War.

Ettore's wife died, then his father, and the Bugatti founder never really recovered. He was no longer at the height of his creative powers and although he was always designing, in truth, compared to the glory days, his final years represent a sad demise, with proposed designs for a fishing boat and a small dinghy never coming to fruition. Ettore even worked on a patent for a gull-wing car, which was sadly never implemented and was eventually superseded by Mercedes' own striking gull-wing, the 300SL, in 1954. Ettore passed away on 21 August 1947 of a lung infection in a military hospital in Paris. Conventional automotive history books tell us that the original Bugatti brand died in the mid-1960s when the brand name was eventually sold off to Hispano-Suiza, an aircraft supplier.

Seeing those historic cars up close, however, tells you so much more. Walking around the museum in Mulhouse was like a genetic 'pick 'n' mix' of Bugatti personality traits. I saw numerous race-winning Bugattis; likewise we saw the last racer to be built in Molsheim from that period, the 1956 Type 251 which had proven to be largely undriveable and a racing failure. I saw the Bugatti 'pick-up', the Type 40 that Ettore had driven across the Sahara to Paris – a journey of 10,000 miles – to prove to a sceptical world that Bugattis were more reliable than their sometimes questionable reputation suggested. It was a three-dimensional walk through the Bugatti history books.

Strolling around the cavernous textile factory in Mulhouse crammed full of classic cars, there were two stars of the show, however: a Type 41 prototype Royale – Ettore Bugatti's personal car – standing grandly on its own podium, looking every bit the legend that it is. And then, in another corner of the vast museum's warehouse, there was a darkened exhibit, pitch black but for a vague silhouette flickering in the darkness. As I walked closer, waves of classical music crashed out of some nearby speakers and, after a thunderclap and some lightning, the Royale's celebrity descendant was thrust into full view by bright spotlights – the oldest surviving Bugatti Veyron prototype. The car was very similar to the eventual production model but I noticed several differences, most obviously the 'holes' in the front of the doors that Dr Schreiber had told me about that afternoon in the workshop. I stood alongside the hushed Japanese journalists and a gaggle of school children as the car revolved on a podium set against footage of its development and captions of the amazing performance statistics. All that was missing was a red carpet.

The overriding feeling that my morning in the museum gave me about Bugatti as a brand (before the Veyron era) was that it was all about creativity, innovation and perhaps, above all, *mystique*. That and the pure fun of driving. Fittingly, perhaps the last words should be left to Julius: 'No other car manufacturer could say they came from a family of artists. Bentley and Porsche and Benz were engineers designing cars. Bugatti was an artist designing cars. This is the secret.'

So now it was my turn to drive to Molsheim, to make the same pilgrimage to the Bugatti factory that Ettore's customers had been making since the last century. Most of them considered it an honour to make the trip and see the factory where their pride and joy was created. OK, we were taking different roads and our chariot was a VW Golf rather than a Royale, but as I approached the town of Molsheim, I felt the same buzz . . . the sense of anticipation was tangible.

As Dr Piëch had pointed out all those years ago, VW's investment in Bugatti was so comprehensive that they had chosen to build this brand-new, 20-acre

In typically innovative style, the entire factory build could be followed online, after Bugatti set up a webcam that streamed footage of the building site itself to their official homepage every three minutes. In all, in excess of 150,000 photos were taken and posted, and at the end of the process these were edited into a time-lapse video that showed the entire construction in just 38 seconds – something which the innovator Ettore would surely have loved? In the footage, cranes, construction lorries, masses of men and hundreds of trucks can be seen ferrying materials and supplies to and from the site in true Benny Hill style, swamping the tiny Alsatian town with a volume of traffic and construction that would normally be more associated with a large city.

state-of-the-art factory and HQ near Molsheim in the same locale as Ettore's original manufacturing base. The actual precise location was in the nearby village of Dorlisheim, close by to Molsheim, and the new factory would rise up 'a stone's throw' from the old sheds where Ettore had built his masterpieces (his family grave is also in Dorlisheim).

The 'Atelier' had been started in the autumn of 2002, with ambitions at that stage to complete the build and begin making the Veyron by the end of 2003. Standing alongside the new space-age factory was the beautiful Château Saint Jean, which VW fully renovated and would use as the offices for the project

The Château St Jean in Molsheim, north-east France.

(there is also a mini-museum there). The outbuildings that could be found on both the western and eastern sides of the Château had originally housed Ettore's racing horses, and these were also rebuilt, precisely to the original plans. No detail was spared. The orangery and old factory gate remain unaltered, original witnesses to the era of Ettore Bugatti.

Building went to plan, despite several last-minute changes, and was ably assisted by long stretches of good Alsatian weather. The renovated sheds and outbuildings, along with the Château, were finished some time before the new-build Atelier, which was eventually 'topped off' at a lavish ceremony in mid-May 2003. Even that had only taken just seven months to complete. On Saturday, 3 September 2005, Bugatti opened the brilliant new factory in front of select guests and the then-president Dr Bscher was clearly buoyed by this latest landmark. Speaking at the event, he said, 'This is where, in 1909, Ettore Bugatti established his company, and where, in 1910, he produced the first automobile bearing his name. And it is on this very spot – and this is a source of great pleasure to me – that his legacy and his philosophy shall live on. We are proud to bring back the Bugatti tradition right here in Molsheim, and we are convinced that we shall be able to continue this tradition in the same sense in which it was intended by its founder.'

The entrance nowadays is somewhat less auspicious than the archway that heralded the founder's factory site. Access is gained via a long stretch of tarmac and another metal barrier arm manned by security guards. A quick left turns you into the car park but as you make the final approach, you can just see the Château in the background, hiding behind the Atelier itself. As my car parked, I noticed two 16.4s resting to the right of the factory, sitting silently in the shadows.

One former stable is now the guest reception area; another stable has been converted into three luxurious guest apartments. A Bugatti Royale can be seen in the background through the double doors.

It is an impressive building, reminiscent perhaps of the best work of Lord Foster and entirely worthy of its subsequent plaudits. Most obviously the oval-shaped Atelier designed by architect Gunter Henn deliberately mimics the famous elliptical Bugatti logo. It is an imposing 76 x 45-metre steel construction that sits in stark contrast to the elaborate and historical château nearby.

First up is coffee in the guest reception area which you walk to via a small hallway . . . in which sits a Bugatti Royale. Once past the near-priceless vintage Bug, we stroll into the reception where beautiful furniture is surrounded by

scale replicas of the cars, an original Veyron wheel, four of the car's seats and an actual Veyron itself. Notably, there is a cable running into the rear of the car, keeping the battery fully charged so that, I sensed, the BV could fire off into the distance at a moment's notice, a small reminder that this was anything but a fashionable ornament. Nearby, books filled with swatches of leather rested on a deeply grained table; it is here that a customer will come to discuss their individual specification, the finer details of their car and the schedule for its delivery. I ask after the rest room and Julius tells me, 'Through the doors, then go past the Royale and turn left.' Did he actually just say that?

The reception is impressive and the Château with its offices and beautiful architecture equally so, but this is not what I really want to see. The Atelier is where I am drawn, the small but mightily impressive workshop where this celebrity is created. It's just a small walk across a gravelled path, past a smattering of small trees where wild deer graze on the grass, and then up a small ramp, finally entering through a large glass door.

As I walked in, I was met by the sight of no fewer than nine Bugatti Veyrons. Three were finished and hiding under immaculate white covers, waiting to be shipped to customers. The rest were in various states of assembly, ranging from two halves of the car that were barely recognisable, to a near-finished Veyron undergoing a rolling road test. To one side is the 2001 Frankfurt prototype – it looked completely different, a bigger but thinner radiator, those holes still in the doors, different wheels, a style study destined for a museum, and not actually a working car.

My first impression inside the Atelier was of almost total quiet. There was no radio, certainly no calendars of semi-naked women and no real noise other than the click of a ratchet, the ping of metal against metal, and occasionally a softly spoken communication between the technicians (they are not called mechanics). The entire room was flooded with natural light from the vast floor-to-ceiling windows on one side and the numerous skylights on the other. The massive windows had vertical, adjustable shades made of perforated metal panels and

The author nosing around the Atelier.

offered a spectacular view of the Vosges Mountains. There was no smell of oil.

There are only ten men who ever work assembling the Veyron and almost all of them have been here since the first car went into assembly back in 2005. One suspects this is not exactly the easiest vacancy to fill, not for want of takers but because the skills needed to put this car together are unique to the project. Each technician wears pristine white gloves at all times and their uniforms are absolutely spotless. Having been inside a modern Formula 1 workshop and factory several times, I'd expected something similar. If anything this was even more clinical, a true automotive laboratory.

A tall man with a shock of hair walked towards me and introduced himself as Fred Schulemann, production director for the Veyron. His suit looked more expensive than my car. He offered to give me a tour of the assembly process and, as I shook his hand, I actually felt guilty for not having had a shower before I walked in. We started chatting, and I first pointed out that just as with Ettore's original factory, initialled tools and benches littered the area. He confirmed that everything had been designed specifically for this workshop, down to the last rack and table. 'This is a link to the history,' suggested Fred. 'Ettore was a very creative man and nothing was good enough for him, so we have done the same.'

Remember, this is not where the parts for the Veyron are actually manufactured, this is an assembly plant. 'We have three streams of assembly,' Fred continued, as we walked towards the far end of the workshop. 'The first phase assembles the engine with the gearbox, the back part of the car. The second part is for the monocoque and the third one is the front end. They are pre-assembled in various locations, using parts from multiple suppliers in many, many countries, and then we marry these three parts together here in this factory.'

When he said 'various locations' he wasn't exaggerating. For example, the wheels were originally cast in Moscow; the monocoque is made in Germany; some surface parts come from Italy; the gearbox is from Ricardo in Bristol and the windscreen glass was originally from Finland, now from Switzerland. The Veyron represents a massive logistical operation.

Assuming this melange of parts from various corners of the globe all arrives on time (and there is a dedicated team of three people at the Atelier to make sure they do), the actual joining of the three pre-assembled sections can begin. Fred continued: 'This is completed in a horizontal way, which is quite different from a normal car assembly. Usually you have a body and you put the engine, the chassis and so on *into* the car. Here we have a horizontal marriage. This is entirely because of the car's concept, we don't have a body, so the Bugatti Veyron is assembled *from the inside out*.' The Veyron does not have a frame for the cockpit like conventional cars; witnessing its assembly here really brings home the strength and ingenuity of the monocoque, which is massively rigid, even though it weighs a mere 108kg. It is reported to be almost triple the strength of a normal car's frame.

Fred talked me through the finer points of the complex marriage, confirming that in essence the actual meeting point for the two halves of the Veyron is held firm by just fourteen titanium bolts. He picked up one of these bolts from a small tub and gave it to me. It felt ludicrously, weirdly light, like plastic to my untrained mind. It is actually as strong as steel but twice as light.

The car's rear frame is initially bolted to the engine and transmission; then the relevant sections are placed – what seems precariously but is of course precisely – on top of steel columns, each embossed on top with the EB logo. These columns are on tracks hidden in the floor and after each part is checked and double-checked, the sections glide across to meet each other. The entire process is by hand, not surprisingly, and the sense of *patience* that exudes from each technician is considerable.

Once the mass of electronics and hydraulics are connected between the respective halves of the car, they push them together and bless the wedding with those fourteen titanium bolts. After countless further checks, the remaining body parts are added only after the strenuous rolling-road test. This includes that mammoth engine being unleashed and the tyres tested at high speed and using 1001bhp. There is also a box to simulate heavy rain and a highlight tunnel that simulates pure sunlight and reveals even the minutest of surface blemishes.

Once fully constructed, each car is then taken outside for an actual road test, some 450 kilometres. Before this is allowed, the entire car is covered with hundreds of transparent film patches to protect it from the grit and elements

outside, even including under the entire wheel arch. Bugatti also use 'test' wheels at this point rather than the customer's own ones. The test itself takes part on a track, the public roads and also at an airport where they test the top speeds. Here, the driver is equipped with a walkie-talkie so that Flight Control can warn him of approaching aeroplanes and he can vacate the spare runway safely.

The process seemed so lengthy, complex and frankly bewildering that to me it felt like each car would be about a year in the making. Fred laughed and explained: 'The whole process is between five and nine weeks, depending on the condition of certain parts. Nearly every part is unique, hand-crafted, you see, and so from time to time it happens that we are not satisfied with the quality of a particular part. If that is the case, then we remove that part and start that section of the assembly from scratch. That means we have to take the car apart and start all over again. I cannot walk into a spares department and pick another part off a shelf. Sometimes, depending on which part is unacceptable, it might be weeks before we get a replacement.'

Fred stopped in front of a particularly striking Veyron. It looked very similar to the mirrored 'piece of art' Veyron I saw all those weeks ago in the Autostadt.

Except unlike that exhibition masterpiece, this car was actually intended to be driven on the road. 'This is a unique car, a customer request,' explained Fred. 'It is polished aluminium, polished so meticulously that it becomes mirrored. This is *very* hard to get right as every tiny blemish, any slight defect shows up. This is probably the most difficult Veyron we have ever had to finish.' It's also one of the most expensive, with the likely eventual cost dwarfing the 'ticket' price. 'It's crucial for us to get such requests absolutely perfect; our customers pay a lot of money for these cars, so we have to be perfect.'

So if I ordered a Veyron today, when could I drive it to my local Sainsbury's? 'Six to nine months, depending on the specification you requested,' explained Fred. He was formerly responsible for the production of Audis in Hungary, where he produced 300 cars a day. This is not Bugatti. The Atelier must be the exact opposite? 'I don't know another plant in the world that is similar to this, it is extraordinary. Outstanding. And yes, it is unusually small.'

At times I feel anxious walking on the shimmering floor. Yet before I was introduced to Fred, I overheard him asking someone to clean a certain corner as he was not satisfied. Like Ettore before them, there is also an element of branding at play here. Each Bugatti customer comes along to see where their car is made. As they cannot physically be present for the entire assembly, it is vital that what they do see is reassuring. 'It has to look perfect for their visits. We need to show how we are working, and the Atelier gives them an impression of our accuracy and perfection, everything is absolutely clean and proper.'

There are various elements of the assembly process that are quite staggering. For example, we stopped at the grille of a Grand Sport and Fred knelt down near the famous enamelled badge, made for the Veyron out of solid silver. This famous oval sports sixty pearl-shapes around the circumference, those stylised initials of the brand's founder Ettore Bugatti, and the word Bugatti on a badge that has adorned each model since 1909.

'If you have a look at the Royale you will see almost the same badge on this car,' explained Fred. 'The Veyron is high technology, very sophisticated, but this badge is made exactly like it was at the time of Ettore, nearly one hundred years ago. We get these from a small German company founded in the 1770s, it is embossed on a machine that is one hundred years old and then after two old women paint this by hand they put it into an oven, after which they grind it by hand many times to perfection. You could buy a small used car for the same price as this enamelled badge.'

But perhaps it is the finish of the carbon fibre body panels that is rather symbolic of the principles at the heart of this operation. Fred explained to me that the dull, lifeless natural colour of carbon fibre is aesthetically utterly unacceptable, so they paint then grind the multiple layers *nine* times. After the eighth painted layer, a 10 per cent tint is added to give the outer panel the final lustrous colour. Most problematic of all, however, is where the thousands of tiny diagonal streams of carbon fibre patterning meet in the middle of the bonnet. I suggest the square-patterned material looks impossible to match up perfectly. 'You're right, it is impossible,' says Fred. 'Well, *almost* impossible.'

Note the word, 'almost'.

WHAT HAS *THIS* BUGATTI DONE FOR BUGATTI?

With the celebrity of the Bugatti Veyron well established, its perhaps tempting to think that relaunching such a prestigious brand was a fait accompli, simply a case of having the big bucks to buy the badge and develop a car. Not so. For the VW group, the Bugatti Veyron was a *big gamble*. Had it failed, as many feared during those turbulent development days, then the rumoured £1.5 billion development cost would have been mightily painful – and embarrassing – for VW to stomach. Just as the Veyron has proved to be a shining example of what the VW group can achieve, conversely had it failed it would have perhaps been the modern car world's most high-profile 'bad review'.

Automotive history is littered with failed attempts at relaunching once-famous car brands. With Bugatti specifically, there was a very recent precedent that had sadly ultimately failed. In 1991 Italian entrepreneur Romano Artioli bought the brand and set up a spectacular factory in Italy, with ambitions of producing a car with remarkably similar performance specifications to the latter-day Veyron. In 1992 the brand had launched the EB110 and its history and spec read like the Veyron of some thirteen years later.

Back then, Bugatti's new owner Artioli wanted to build the most technically advanced supercar ever – just like his VW counterparts did with the Veyron. Again, like the Veyron, his team created brand-new techniques, including one of the first-ever carbon fibre monocoque chassis in a road car, using technology originally developed on French space rockets. It was four-wheel drive and there were four turbochargers too, as with the Veyron, again a first. The early 1990s design even had a speed-sensitive rear wing for high speed, just like the Veyron. The price? £281,000, which in today's money is about £500,000 (albeit some way short of the Veyron's hefty price tag). The acceleration was 0–60 in 3.2 seconds compared to the Veyron's 2.5 seconds but at the time this still made it the fastest supercar in the world. And yes, they also called the extreme model 'Super Sport' too. The EB110 moniker was to commemorate the 110th anniversary of Ettore's birth.

'Artioli: A great character, a great gentleman but what a task!' enthused Bugatti historian Julius Kruta when I asked him about the Italian predecessor to the Veyron. 'He bought the name from Snecma who were producing parts for the aero industry, such as on the Airbus and Concorde, at the Bugatti factory in Molsheim. The Bugatti name was still strong and Artioli fulfilled his dream of building a Bugatti in Italy in that Bermuda triangle round Modena where Ferrari, Lamborghini, Maserati and now Pagani and others reside.'

The factory that Artioli built was also mightily impressive: the main building was a large round tower with a hanging roof. The lower area was a convention and presentation area, while the upper floor contained absolutely state-of-the-art engineering offices with breathtakingly beautiful wooden floors. The production hall itself was also very upmarket, flooded with natural light and very impressive. The huge lawns were bordered by fabulous fences all proudly emblazoned with the EB logo. It was as much a marketing triumph as a manufacturing base. The striking design of the car's exterior was penned by Marcello Gandini who is the man responsible for the Lamborghini Countach and Lancia Stratos, and came complete with futuristic scissor doors. When the car was launched on Ettore Bugatti's birthday in 1991, the motoring world watched with baited breath.

Unfortunately, the EB110 ultimately failed for several reasons. Most obviously, the economic climate was entirely unwelcoming for selling a car with such a price tag; the global recession of 1990/1991 had crippled many countries and disposable income, even of the super-wealthy, was restricted (although Michael Schumacher was one famous owner). Supercar prices were tumbling. In the same period, marques such as Rolls-Royce reportedly saw their sales drop by up to 50 per cent. Secondly, Artioli's independent status proved just how difficult it is to develop a new car in the modern era without the backing of a major group.

Artioli intended to sell a high number of EB110s but in the end the figure stalled around 140. He'd sunk a substantial amount of his own money – and passion – into the project and to many people had created a hugely impressive piece of engineering. The EB110 was a car very much ahead of the game. But it was destined for the history books only; after presenting a very intriguing four-door concept car at Geneva in 1993 which was beautifully designed and reminiscent of several classic Bugattis, Artioli's company went bust. The Bugatti dream was in tatters again.

Going back further, cars were even produced in the classic Bugatti years that have been seen by some as 'flops'. Perhaps of all the glorious Bugattis, the most obviously 'prestigious' was the legendary Royale. This gigantic car – almost six metres long with an 8-cylinder engine generating 300bhp and a speed of 200km/h was a work of beauty. Just six of the 'Type 41' – as it was officially named – were made, with grand ambitions of the Royale becoming 'the car of kings'.

However, despite the vehicle's regal name and stately presence, no royal figurehead ever actually owned one and only three were commercially sold. Like the EB110, the car emerged just as the world plunged into an economic crisis, in the Royale's case the Great Depression which started in 1929. Some have called the Royale one of the car world's greatest flops. As I noted earlier, however, in a sense the Royale was anything but because the car's technology later secured Bugatti the lucrative contract to build engines for the French national railway. Nonetheless, the historical risks of launching a car were all too familiar to Bugatti and VW.

One final reason to question the wisdom of the Veyron project was VW's own financial position in the late 1990s. Although development costs for a new family car are often in the region of several billion pounds, that is for volume production whereas the £1.5 billion needed for the Veyron was initially to produce only 300 coupes. So it was clear that for all their corporate clout, VW were taking a big risk. The question is, has it paid off?

As an exercise in branding, the Bugatti Veyron is a prestige masterclass. Amidst all the talk of cars that cost £5 million and sell for 'just' £1 million, it's never easy to forget exactly what the project has created in terms of remarkable PR. The Veyron's chief engineer Dr Schreiber had seemed very conscious of the brand when I'd met him. He frequently said the words, 'This is Bugatti', while highlighting various parts, obviously aware that the Veyron wasn't just a technical exercise but also a lavish and scintillating branding triumph perhaps without peer in recent automotive history.

But who better to quiz about the car's worth to the brand than the outgoing president of Bugatti, Dr Franz-Josef Paefgen. I had arranged to meet him at a very exclusive private club in Knightsbridge, nestled away from the main road where every five minutes a supercar or high-end marque will inevitably be spotted heading down to Harrods or a multimillion-pound apartment. As I waited for his arrival in a small meeting room which had a one-way glass wall overlooking the kitchens, I noticed a signed bottle of wine whose label carried a picture of a Formula 1 car made by a 'rival' brand. I turned the picture to face the wall, chuckling as I did.

Dr Paefgen was exactly on time, despite having had an extensive day of meetings, and his presence filled the small meeting room instantly. Chatting with him and looking back over the Veyron project was a fascinating way to summarise and place so many issues in context. He was repeatedly at pains to stress how crucial Dr Neumann had been to the project and that much of the work had already been completed when he became president. First I wanted to know a little more about the boy that had become the president: 'My father was self-employed with his own unbranded workshop, in those days that was a profitable business although we were not a very rich family. It had started off after the war when he used to take three or four wrecked cars and make them into one new car which you then could sell and make a little bit of money.'

So cars were a major part of your childhood? 'I have been a car nut for as long as I can remember. In those days, half the world was Beetles, the other half was probably Mercedes. I had posters of both on my bedroom wall. Later the [Mercedes] 300SL too, although no Bugattis! Then when I was fourteen I made the decision that I wanted to become a car engineer; I worked in a workshop, then studied at university and eventually became a graduate trainee at Ford. At that point, my dream was always to become a department manager. At Ford I had a boss who earned DM100,000, had a big Ford Granada company car and went home every day at 5 o'clock. To me at that age, that seemed like a good combination!'

So what did your father's workshop teach you? 'I saw the cars that customers were buying and bringing in. The workshop was in the middle of the city so a lot of customers came and dropped their car off in the morning, we did some work on it during the day and they took the car back in the evening. I saw so many customers and that is the basis for my marketing knowledge today; I gained a very good understanding of which customer drives what car and *why*. So the lawyer had a dark blue Mercedes Benz, the butcher had a 300S and so on. You learned to read the customer's preferences. The difficulty was always: would they change the brand? And normally they would not.'

With this brand intransigency in mind, the relaunch of Bugatti was a daunting risk. Although Dr Paefgen stressed again that he had not been president at the relaunch, it was clear that his vast knowledge of car history had made him all too aware of the challenge: 'There was virtually no Bugatti. As a teenager I went to circuits where Graham Hill and Jim Clark raced and so compared to cars like the Lotus 25, Bugatti was nothing. It was only after I had finished my studies that I gained an understanding of the fantastic engineering and craftsmanship in all these early Bugattis. But there were no cars on the road and there was no nice emotional car to look at.'

Dr Paefgen also offered me a fascinating insight into the enigmatic Dr Piëch, the man behind the original idea for the Veyron: 'The origin of the project is Piëch, who in his understanding as an engineer always tries to go for the *extreme*. If there is a very fuel-efficient car, he wants to do the *most* fuel-efficient car; if there is a fast car, he wants to do the *fastest* car. He always loved to have that challenge as an engineer. "Where is the top? Let's go for the top."

'Knowing Herr Piëch pretty well, the Veyron is a typical Piëch car because he is totally dedicated to engineering challenges and I think he needed the singular challenge to build the best car in the world. In his head, I can see exactly where it came from. First of all, it was clearly derived from his Le Mans experience. He was involved in developing the Porsche 917 which had more than 1000bhp and was one of the few race cars that could run at [close to or above] 400km/h on the straight; so he knew what he was talking about, he had done a 1000-horsepower engine before, he had done a 400km/h car before, therefore I can see him thinking, *Let's bring both together and make it a driveable car.*

'So now the key was to find a brand and a car where that concept would fit properly and could then be sold as a top product of the VW group. We as engineers were absolutely convinced that the Veyron was a crazy project. I think the initial comments were, "Now Piëch's completely gone! We knew he always came up with extreme ideas but this . . . ?" So when I came to the project, I just watched carefully what was going on and after not too long I thought to myself, *Yes, we were right, this* is *a crazy project.*'

The infamous delays meant that when Dr Paefgen became president, many insiders felt the job was a poisoned chalice: 'Dr Neumann had clearly designed a proper engine which did deliver what everybody expected. It had beautiful styling by Herr Warkuss, a wonderful engine and a good transmission concept, but a lot of the details were just not right in the concept phase and the car didn't work at the time they wanted it to go to market. The car did not make the progress they wanted to see.

'As with many projects, you immediately think about the risks and all the difficulties you might face. But at the same time, as an engineer, I thought, *Oh wow, that is something. 1000 horsepower, 400km/h, this is something that's never been done before.* I had been working on, for example, an Audi A2 that only used three litres of fuel per 100 kilometres, and I'd previously been involved in work on Lamborghinis, but never something that was as extreme as this car.'

Once installed as the new CEO of Bugatti Engineering (and later president), Dr Paefgen's focus quickly became apparent and the path to an eventual successful launch became clearer: 'The most important thing I needed at that time was a young, powerful engineer, which was Schreiber who was the expert for transmissions in the group. Then of course there were a few more normal things, we needed a few more people, facilities, a little bit of money, a little bit of time. The rest was not so difficult. I think Wolfgang Schreiber was the difficult piece of the jigsaw because nobody wanted to let him go as a transmission expert, but after a few weeks that was agreed and we could start our work.'

But as a *brand*, did you not feel that VW were taking an enormous risk?

'There are a few very simple facts and answers. There have been cars at Le Mans that have done 400km/h before and so physically there was no reason why it should not happen. I viewed it in engineering terms. Is the engine powerful enough? Are the wheels and tyres doing the job? At the same time, when taking over responsibility [for the Veyron] I was of course walking into Nowhere Land where nobody had been before. So yes, at the end of the day there was the question: how big is the risk you are taking trying to build such a car?'

Dr Paefgen knows and respects Mr Artioli – the man behind the failed early 1990s bid to relaunch Bugatti – very well, and had even travelled many times to the latter's beautiful factory in Modena. But Paefgen was still undeterred by the brand's immediate precedent, despite the obvious severity of the challenges.

'When we started the job we were definitely not absolutely sure that we could do it. Because there had been very good engineers working on the project and they had problems, they were struggling and everybody was aware of that. I had obviously seen the statements in the public that the car would go into production on a certain day and then it didn't happen and then there was another delay, so everybody was aware that there were problems. So my first reaction was, *Why should I be able to do something they have not been able to do over the last two or three years?* I think it was only after the first analysis [with Dr Schreiber] that we saw a reason why they had been struggling and also a clear way to success. And since then there was a lot of confidence [growing] and it worked, it actually evolved step by step and we finally made it happen.'

When the car had finally been made ready to launch, Dr Paefgen was very keen to make sure its presentation was perfect; he knew the engineering was exemplary but as president he was also aware that as a brand, this was perhaps the most crucial moment: 'The question was, "What is the story that we are telling the world?" A lot of stories had already been told. As a concept the car was already very well known to the world.'

This included some not very positive preconceptions: 'At the beginning everybody said the car was just for going straight ahead and nothing else, but in testing we had found out that it was a lot more capable than that. So we decided that there was a story to tell about the other capabilities of the car rather than just going 400. For example, my personal view is that one of the most impressive experiences in a Veyron is the braking, this air brake coming up; in every other powerful sports car when you brake hard you always have the dynamic effect that the rear end comes up a little bit and makes the car lighter. Not in the Veyron. The air brake creates a wonderful and very safe feeling, therefore driving fast and braking hard becomes a pleasure and not something to fear any more.

'So we planned to do the press launch in Sicily and we consciously chose roads which were not perfectly straight, but twisty roads that demanded lots of

accelerate-brake, accelerate-brake. We knew that in the Veyron this would be like dancing.'

But superficially, the car world kept focusing on the top speed; so how did Dr Paefgen and the brand get around this? 'Driving 400 is a challenge but driving at such speed is never without any risk, if something is wrong with the car or maybe a tyre, there will not be much left of the car. So we came to the conclusion that rather than doing a big event where everybody could try to drive 400 (which would add to the risk), we decided to do the top-speed story before we launched the car in Sicily. So we invited a European and an American journalist to do the 400, which they both did. So then the 400 story was out and we could concentrate on the actual full launch.

'That press launch in Sicily was a wonderful event. We had an old Bugatti, two old 35 Formula 1 cars, the Veyrons there, it was fabulous. Many journalists actually got lost in the car, they actually just drove and drove and drove and didn't want to come back! It was a small event but it made a very strong impact.' (Dr Schreiber had concurred when we spoke about the launch previously: 'Every evening [during the launch] we had a press conference and the journalists always asked us why the car was so expensive, so much more than all the other super sports cars. Then, when they'd had the chance to drive the car, they didn't question that again because they understood why the price was different because the car is completely different.')

With the car out in the open, the brand challenges were not over, however.

'Those who judge the value of an automobile by its outer appearance and the quality of its surface, will most probably not be tempted to buy a Bugatti. The maker of this small car has, indeed, not made the slightest effort to compete with those popular and inexpensive car models that are to already to be found on the market. The fact of the matter is, that the price to be paid for a Bugatti is considerably higher than for any other car of the same category. The reason for this is that this production represents an entirely new class by itself.'
English journalist W. F. Bradley writing for *The Motor* magazine in 1910, the very first article about Bugatti.

Dr Paefgen: 'Selling the car is another challenge. You cannot just open a showroom and wait for customers to come by. And also you can't offer a test drive to everybody who is interested. So you need to develop a system to identify the potential customers and then create events where these few customers can come along and enjoy the car.'

There was no precedent for selling 300 units at €1 million or more each. The McLaren F1 had an initial run of 40 cars with 106 ultimately being made; insiders suggested they'd originally had designs on selling 350. The doomed EB110 is cited as a flop but actually managed to sell around 140 cars in a time of economic crisis which was a remarkable achievement. Other select supercars are also very limited – the Enzo, the Carrera GT, the F40 were all produced in very low numbers, but also at considerably lower prices. Most recently the Lamborghini Reventon, a fighter-jet-inspired version of the LP640 model, sold out of its limited run in hours, but only twenty of these $1 million cars were made. Selling 300 cars at this seven figure price? . . . this was uncharted territory.

'That was a big challenge [for the brand]. We'd had a lot of comments that at that price we would probably sell 100, and some said if we worked really hard we might sell 150, but never 300. Our problem was that we had to agree with the numerous suppliers on a production quantity in order to make the numbers work. So Wolfgang Schreiber and myself had a meeting and – although not fully agreed by the sales and marketing guys at that time – we put a number of 300 in. There was a very real risk that if 300 was too many, we'd have to scrap [some very expensive] parts at the end of the day, but we thought the [brand] risk was a lot worse to produce 150 cars and then find 100 customers who couldn't get a car.'

As this book goes to press, Bugatti informed me that they have sold all 300 coupes. Which brings me to the urban myth that each Veyron costs £5 million and therefore makes a huge loss to the VW group. 'The financial side I can explain in a very simple way,' said Dr Paefgen enthusiastically. 'Considering the very small volume we are producing, as soon as you start to allocate all the fixed costs and all the initial investment to the cars you are financially dead, of course. Because having this wonderful château, the new production facilities in Molsheim, the development of the car, this is just a very expensive effort. We agreed finally that we would write off all the initial investment and just do a simple calculation with costs per car and income per car and, based on that, the car is clearly positive, so every car we built adds to the profit of the company. Secondly, this is a long-term marketing investment into the brand and I'm pretty sure you could sell the Bugatti brand by now with a lot of added value attached.

'Also, and this is crucial to this conversation, Piëch had this simple saying, "The Veyron is our Formula 1." If you consider the cost of a Formula 1 team, it used to be around €700 million, that is a lot money. What is that? Marketing money? Engineering money? In the same way, a lot of the work and ideas we have developed on the Veyron will, one way or another, come back to other production cars. For example, the carbon ceramic brakes we introduced with the Veyron are now in some Lamborghinis, Bentleys, Audis and VWs.'

As Dr Paefgen suggested, the technological advancements made during the Veyron's development might initially be used on that car but will inevitably trickle down through the entire VW empire and thereafter across commercial car manufacturers in general, to the benefit of all. This filtering down of high-end technology from projects like the Veyron is what Bugatti have themselves termed 'cross-brand synergy effects', which in essence means you will find more modest versions of the same technological ideas in cars made by the VW group, such as Volkswagen, Audi, Skoda and Seat.

And of course, the Veyron will not be the last car that Bugatti makes. At the time of writing, there is widespread speculation about Bugatti's next move. The brand has confirmed the development of a four-door saloon car, internally called Galibier. Their stated ambition with this new car is to achieve something

The Bugatti Galibier.

as outstanding and unique in the world of four-door cars as the Veyron is among the super sports cars. 'Or, if you like, just as the Type 41 Royale was in its time.' There are other projects, such as the Rembrandt, a concept car which is expected to appear in the next few years. And most pertinent for this book, there is a new Veyron concept too. Secretive development of this has yielded few tips as to what to expect, but motoring magazines suggest the car will exceed the world record held by the Super Sport. The concept car is expected to appear around 2013.

On wider issues, some critics will rail against what the brand appears to champion; cars like the Veyron will always attract derisory comments and some critics argue that as very few people can afford cars like the Veyron, this in some ways makes them pointless, or somehow lessens their achievement. This is spurious because for the average man on the street, a car in excess of perhaps £40–50K is often unobtainable, so if we apply that logic then a huge slew of supercars and indeed top-of-the-range 'everyday' cars are also pointless.

In fact, part of the appeal of the Veyron – and indeed any cars of that ilk – is precisely that they *are* unobtainable to the majority. That elusive quality is what adds to the aura around the car; just as with ultra-talented celebrities, there is something 'other-worldly' about them. The word 'normal' is a very nebulous term but the countless celebrities I have come into contact with almost universally display some characteristic, personality trait, drive, ambition, talent or foible that is not typical of the wider population. In my experience, they are not 'normal' people; ditto the Veyron.

The polluting properties of the brand's car do not make Bugatti popular with the environmentalist lobby. Nobody ever expected the Veyron to be economical on fuel, of course. There's really no argument against this either, save for pointing out that with a total of 450 cars being manufactured, although each particular car is poor in terms of emissions, they are at least limited to those small number of units. For sure the mass volumes of VWs, Toyotas, Fords and so on are causing far more damage to the global ecology, but let's not pretend that the Veyron is really green. It isn't.

However, in terms of pure branding, has the Veyron been a success? 'One thing you should never forget is that this car is a flagship for the VW group and it provides very strong proof of the technological capabilities of the whole company. Everybody is now aware that the VW group is not just capable of building the car with the highest volume in the world but also the car with the greatest technology in the world.

'If you compare making supercars with mountain climbing, well before the Veyron everybody was in the Alps climbing up to 4000 metres, and then suddenly we said, "We've been to 8000 metres!" The car was so far ahead of everybody else. It still is. We are now more than ten years since the concept was announced to the public, yet still to this day nobody else is even close.'

Dr Paefgen is clearly fiercely proud of the Veyron. Yet when I ask him the final question, 'Looking back, how did you do it?' he reveals a streak of humility which, in the context of exactly what that car represents, is entirely surprising and rather refreshing: 'What we did was just the normal engineering work. What is the problem? Is there a solution or is there a way round? Who would be able to help us and is knowledgeable enough to be able to contribute to the problem? Let's do a concept, produce some parts, test it and then see if it works. It was not rocket science.'

There are perhaps two specific ways of placing the Veyron's achievements in context: firstly, how does the car sit among its contemporaries, namely, how does it stand up against other supercars? And secondly, as a piece of engineering, what is its place in the modern firmament of engineering feats?

Taking the context of the Veyron within the modern supercar echelon first, it is clear that Bugatti's achievement has dwarfed its competitors. The Veyron has comprehensively moved the goalposts, so demonstrably that it appears – for now at least – others seem reluctant to take up the baton. Some have even suggested that the Veyron's triumph is so complete that it will be the last internal-combustion-engine car that achieves such performance.

Where rival firms do deign to compete, it is rarely on the same scale. Ferrari seem decidedly muted. On the one hand they recently launched what might just be the most stylish Ferrari of the modern era – the stunning and brutally fast 458 Italia – yet on the other, in certain areas of performance they seemed to be withdrawing from the arena altogether. It's perhaps no coincidence that in early 2010 Ferrari's chief executive Amedeo Felisa declared that his company were no longer interested in such extravagant top speeds. 'Top speed is not important to us any more.' Maybe that day when the Veyron had dashed down the Autobahn with Dr Schreiber followed by Dr Paefgen in the Enzo had been a symbolic moment for both companies?

Some car experts argue that elements of technology in the new McLaren MP4-12C (launched in early 2011) compete with the brains in the Veyron. When the car was launched, McLaren supremo and Veyron denigrator Ron Dennis perhaps made a veiled hint that he was coming after the Bugatti, at

least in terms of innovation: 'We respect and admire our competitors in the high-performance sports car market, just as we do in the world of Formula 1, but I also believe that fierce competition drives technology and innovation and produces ever better products. It is our philosophy to push what is possible in car design and engineering and bring innovation and engineering excellence to the performance-car world.' Ron Dennis and the Veyron had history: in 2010 Mr Dennis spoke about the Bugatti in far from flattering terms in an interview for *Arabian Business*, calling it a 'piece of junk' and 'pig ugly' and saying there was not one element of the car that made him feel good.

There is, in this author's opinion, only one car that can even pretend to compete with the Bugatti Veyron and that is Gordon Murray's mythical McLaren F1 from 1992. High-profile criticism aside, it is with the MP4-12C's famous predecessor that the true context of the Veyron can be brought into sharper focus.

The McLaren and the Veyron are two machines separated by thirteen years yet they remain comic-book rivals, the two poster dream cars that we all want in our Top Trumps hand of cards. The rivalry as such was heightened by a very famous interview with Gordon Murray ahead of the Veyron's release when he said, 'The most pointless exercise on the planet has got to be this four-wheel-drive thousand-horsepower Bugatti. I think it's incredibly childish this thing people have about just one element – top speed or standing kilometre or 0–60. It's about as narrow-minded as you can get as a car designer to pick on one element. That's not car designing – that just reeks of a company who are paranoid.' (Note: when Murray eventually drove the Veyron for *Road and Track* magazine in 2008, he was considerably more complimentary, calling the engine 'an engineering wonder').

Gordon Murray was a Formula 1 race car designer and engineer who was challenged with designing a monumental machine – in his own words, the F1 was intended to be the ultimate motoring experience, the closest a car buyer could get to a street-legal grand prix car. This was a car that was all about no compromise. It dripped with cutting-edge technology and, yes, the underside of the bulkhead was lined in gold, as this was considered the best conductor of heat.

The performance was stunning (0–60 in 3.2 seconds and a top speed of 240mph, a world record at the time) and designer Peter Stevens' beautiful lines are still some of the finest ever to bedeck a supercar. The no-compromise ethic was paramount so no traction control, no launch control, no power steering, no anti-lock brakes, no plush carpets, few mod cons. And finally there was the cost: at the time of launch the F1 cost an enormous £634,500 plus VAT.

For all of the 1990s and the first half of the 2000s, the F1 was untouched as the greatest supercar of them all. The car has long been heralded as the ultimate purist's car, a stripped-back, no-frills racing experience on the road;

The McLaren F1: An unrestricted top speed of 240mph made it the fastest road car of all time. The sprint from 0–60 came along in just 3.2 seconds. This was an unheard of combination. The car boasted a 6.1-litre quad-cam V12 BMW engine which generated 627bhp, dwarfing its contemporaries and creating more torque than a Formula 1 engine. Its prodigiously lightweight construction (Murray targeted only a tiny 1000kg and almost hit that figure) made powerful cars such as the blisteringly quick Porsche 959 and Ferrari F40 look flabby. The Formula 1-style carbon-composite construction helped too. The weight distribution was assisted by having the driver's seat in the centre of the car, sandwiched between and slightly ahead of the two passenger buckets on either side. The dihedral doors were the stuff of spaceships.

as we know, the Veyron has by contrast comfortable leather seats, a CD player, air-conditioning, all the mod cons. I'd been lucky enough to be a passenger in two celebrity clients' F1s, and I can still vividly recall the brutal acceleration and impressive presence of both those magnificent cars. I am a huge F1 fan but I prefer the Veyron; which car you prefer essentially comes down to subjective opinion because in terms of pure statistics there is no comparison. Setting aside for a moment the personal preference of 'race car purity versus driveability' that is at the heart of any comparison between an F1 and a Veyron, the pure statistical comparison is startlingly in favour of the Bugatti.

A full 0.7 seconds quicker to 60mph, the Veyron then brutally continues this speed superiority. It reaches 100mph in 4.94 seconds, nearly 1.5 seconds faster than the F1; 150mph comes along in less than 10 seconds, while the F1 'languishes' behind taking 12.8 seconds.

If you perform a straight drag race between an F1 and a Veyron, the Bugatti will be able to get to 200mph and then back to a complete standstill before the F1 has reached 200. You can let the F1 get to 120mph before the Veyron even starts and it will *still* get to 200mph at the same time. And here's another comparison: in the same time that it takes an F1 to accelerate to 200mph, the Veyron Super Sport can get to 200, then brake back to zero . . . *and then accelerate back up to 60mph again*.

As much as I love the F1 and am thrilled to have been driven in it, I never personally understood the 'race car for the road' ethos. I know the F1 is indeed a masterpiece, and likewise the Ferrari F40, but when I hear of Porsche replacing the badge on the nose of their GTs with a sticker to make it lighter, I just don't get it. I know why, I understand the approach and application, stripping out carpets,

The Veyron's bewildering speed superiority was presented brilliantly by *Top Gear* in Series 13 when the team flew to Abu Dhabi to perform a straight drag race against the F1. *Top Gear* notably rolled out the red carpet for the Veyron and the tests they conducted are among some of the show's finest moments, including racing a Cessna 182 light aircraft across Europe, a head-to-head with a fighter jet and a competition against a Pagani Zonda F.

Here, Jeremy Clarkson presents Pierre-Henri Raphanel with the trophy for 'Car of the Year 2010'.

door panels, no mod cons, lighter engine parts etc. But it's not an approach I prefer.

OK, so being able to ferry food back from the supermarket was never really a parameter for supercar analysis, but I'm exaggerating to make a point. How can it be considered easier to produce a car for the road that is essentially a modified race car, than it is a car for the road that is equally (or more) fast yet can indeed be used every day? Purists argue the latter isn't the purpose or raison d'être of a 'proper' supercar, that somehow the 'super' part is diluted by the air-con and radio, ease of use and carpets, door handles and so on. I just don't agree but ultimately it's a subjective standpoint, of course, and no one is right or wrong. It's a personal preference. For me, if I've just spent the best part of a million quid on a car, I'd at least want some carpet. Maybe it was the lush 'velour' trim in my Marina estate that set the trend.

Getting back to those comparative statistics between the F1 and the Veyron, the fact that not even the brilliant and historically important F1 can hold a candle to a Veyron truly gives you some sense of just how far Bugatti advanced supercar performance. Maybe it was rocket science after all?

This brings us to the second contextual way of looking at the Veyron's achievements which is, as mentioned, 'Where does it stand in more general engineering terms?' Such was the fascination with the Veyron's development that even before it had been officially launched and in fact was in the midst of relentless industry rumours that all was not necessarily going to plan, the car had won its first award. Or at least, the Bugatti brand won an award. The

Automobilclub von Deutschland awarded its 'Innovations Prize' to the brand as recognition of the ambition and vision they had displayed by bringing the brand back to life and in such an emphatic and innovative fashion.

This award highlighted the same 'Concorde moment' that *Top Gear*'s own Jeremy Clarkson would talk about when he finally tested the car on his show. His programme also lavished trophies on the car: in December 2005 the vehicle received two awards including 'Car of the Year' and the 'Dream Car of the Year'. He also said, 'Other cars are small guesthouses on the front at Brighton and the Bugatti is the Burj Al Arab. It makes even the Enzo and the Porsche Carrera GT feel slow and pointless. It is a triumph for lunacy over common sense, a triumph for man over nature and a triumph for Volkswagen over absolutely every other car maker in the world.' This was quite a turnaround for Bugatti; the English press had initially been the most sceptical in the troublesome development days. But once the Veyron finally arrived and delivered on its promises, they have since been perhaps the most supportive of all the international press.

The Veyron was a car designed around a vision, without consideration for the limitations of money, existing engineering, commerce or environmental parameters. And in so doing, the Veyron project could already be seen to have contributed to automotive technology, despite not yet being a commercially available vehicle. The Automobilclub von Deutschland stated, 'The new Bugatti is a vision which, thanks to a large number of innovations, has become one of the best automobiles ever built. Anyone who would argue with reason alone has not understood that the realisation of innovations is a question of vision, resulting from a tolerance for fantasy and creativity. An abundance of solutions provide a powerful impulse and the courage to move beyond new frontiers, so that distant goals can become attainable.' The institution went on to applaud Bugatti for giving 'their employees an extreme amount of freedom to develop to the best they were able, without asking if and when all of the efforts would finally pay off. This prize is therefore a salute to entrepreneurial courage in a time in which wavering and half-hearted notions are all too common.'

'Entrepreneurial courage' is the prime mover behind many great engineering feats. What Bugatti have done with the Veyron is altered the accepted parameters of car manufacture, an industry that was already over a century old when they first began their dream. As such, that grandiose ambition legitimately links them to numerous ancestral engineering forefathers, as well as a host of contemporaries in unrelated industries.

For example, bridge building has a long and illustrious past with Roman architects constructing viaducts and bridges principally from stone, some examples of which still exist today. In the twelfth century, the original London bridge picked up on some of these Roman ideas, specifically the use of arches,

'Men who had grown old in the trade could not believe their eyes . . . Visitors were awed. Maria Edgeworth noted: "Machinery so perfect appears to act with the happy certainty of instinct and the foresight of reason combined."' A contemporary journalist reflecting on Sir Mark Isambard Brunel's ship-rigging technology, rather than a car reviewer talking about the Veyron.

but modified them extensively, even boasting houses on the bridge itself. Perhaps the most exhilarating era of bridge building came during the Industrial Revolution when engineers took several historically proven aspects of bridge building and complemented this with revolutionary new materials and design concepts. The 'blue riband' bridge in this arena was constructed in 1779 across the River Severn in the idyllic English county of Shropshire. The 100-foot bridge was built by Abraham Darby just downstream from Coalbrookdale, itself a world-leading literal and metaphorical furnace for iron ore smelting technology. Cantilever and suspension bridges would later extend the capabilities of bridges to unthinkable lengths.

This firebrand thinking can be found at the heart of similar 'great leaps' in areas such as sewerage (Bazalgette's London system), ship-building (Isambard Kingdom Brunel's iron globe-trotting behemoth the SS *Great Eastern*), waterways (the illiterate James Brindley's Worsley–Manchester canal, the Panama canal), railways (the Pacific Railroad, the Trans-Siberian Railway), tunnelling (the Thames tunnel, the Chunnel), energy collection (the Hoover Dam) and so on. In most of these cases, previous systems and efforts existed or had been speculated upon; what these projects did, however, was push the technology and ambition to new heights, in fact to such a degree that they were almost reinventing the solution altogether.

There are three relevant and important points when discussing these remarkable achievements in the context of the Veyron. Firstly, what drove all these engineering feats to success was vision. Sometimes this was a singular, almost fanatical ambition (such as with Thomas Telford, Brunel et al.) while other times it was a combined effort that broke the mould. Secondly, achieving this vision required an almost blinkered self-belief in all cases, a refusal to accept the established convention, a vivid ability to create ideas and methods that had not been tried before. These landmark achievements all came many years after the first examples of their industry yet each project decided that there was perhaps a better approach to numerous long-standing challenges. And thirdly, each achievement not only pushed the boundaries of what had previously been established convention, but they all individually opened the way to an acceleration of development, whether that was an explosion of metal bridges, a mass adoption of underground sewage systems, industrial expansion due to better transport links, and so on. Landmark moments in engineering are not exclusively the first historical spark of invention.

Sir Norman Foster, architect of the Millau viaduct in France, the highest and longest in the world, described his creation as 'impossibly delicate'; twenty years of investigation into the idea of tunnelling an underwater connection between France and England 'entirely convinced the French Channel Tunnel directors that, practically speaking, a tunnel is impossible'; early iron ship-building was laborious and slow to progress, with engineers principally grappling with the strength and weight issues – take this extract from a paper in the *Journal of the Society of Arts* from December 1858: 'Mr Lloyd suggested that one thick plate would answer better. He sent the contractors to ask whether they could make these large four-inch plates. They said it was impossible, but nevertheless, if they were ordered, they would do it, and they did it as a matter of course.' Travelling above the speed of sound in a plane was also, for most of Concorde's development, considered impossible. That word again.

Likewise, when looking at the seemingly 'impossible' challenges presented to the Veyron team and its subsequent mind-boggling performance capabilities, surely the Bugatti deserves its place in this prestigious hall of engineering fame?

Stripping all these lofty comparisons back and looking at the very core of what the Veyron represents, I am reminded of that Countach poster I had on my bedroom wall as a boy, just as Dr Schreiber had his 911 poster and Dr Paefgen had a picture of the gull-wing Mercedes on his bedroom wall. Each night when I read stories to my eight-year-old, I do so while being looked down upon by a large-format poster of the 16.4 from *Top Gear Turbo* magazine. And that's what Bugatti and their team did for the brand when they made the Veyron. They created a legend.

CHAPTER FOURTEEN

LIVING WITH A CELEBRITY

We've seen how the Bugatti Veyron came about, how it was developed, manufactured, launched, how it broke records and ultimately how it became a modern-day celebrity. But there is one final question to ask in this quest. What is it actually like to own one?

Bugatti have an elite network of just 35 dealerships globally. Jack Barclay, the only official Bugatti dealership in the UK (and a partner of the brand for decades) seemed like the best place to ask these questions. Their showroom is very understated, behind a secured grilled fence and out of sight down a near-invisible cul-de-sac in Mayfair. Access through the locked gate leads you down

a small ramp and into a beautifully simple subterranean showroom, filled with a dream car collection, including several Lambos, a Rolls-Royce and an Aston Martin among others. Yet even here, in a room filled with modern supercars and vintage racers, all gleaming and stunning, there is a far corner of the showroom cordoned off for two particular cars. The VIPs in question who need this roped off area? A Veyron 16.4 and a Grand Sport.

I was greeted by an immaculately dressed salesman called Jeremy Mitchell. I'd already tried – and failed – to phone up and arrange to test drive a Veyron. Assuming that Jeremy was comfortable that the prospective buyer on the phone was genuine, what would happen next? 'You need to find out more about the client and his background especially related to cars. And also how much knowledge they have about Bugatti, if they are serious they would have done their homework; are they after a Grand Sport, a coupe, a new or used car? Specific colours, maybe they've been to the factory or Geneva, maybe their friend has one.'

I'd assumed he would run a pretty invasive financial check at this early stage: 'No, if the phone went now, I'd have an initial informal chat and at the end of the conversation and through speaking to people every day that buy cars, that will give me an informed start. If any alarm bells rang, I would – through

Two Veyrons roped off at HR
Owen in central London.

due diligence – do background checks.' Although Jeremy did not mention this,
one aspect that Bugatti – just like any supercar dealer – like to look out for is so-
called 'flippers', people who buy a sought-after car (with a long waiting list) and
then resell it soon after for profit.

But presumably going out for a jolly in a million-pound car is something a
lot of people will chance their arm on? 'Not often. Because first you have to be
quite brazen and it will come out in the wash pretty quickly. Plus, we rarely do
test drives in that car. In order to do a test drive we have to have completed a full
background check. Bugatti is obviously a very exclusive brand and the car is of a
very high value. In order for us and Bugatti to be happy that the potential person
is genuine about buying the car, we have to go through an authorisation check
with the factory before we can take the car out.'

So what is the next step? 'Subject to Bugatti themselves being happy with

all the information we have given them, we would arrange for the potential customer to go to the factory in Molsheim. That's a big commitment [to travel to France].'

And apart from seeing the factory, why test in France? 'Imagine test driving a Veyron in London! It's not the ideal environment to get the best out of the car. As a salesman you have to bear in mind that there is quite a sizable liability involved. You can't really justify a test drive in London. However, it would give you an idea of how well the car performs in traffic!'

What happens when they get to Molsheim? 'They are invited into the customer area where they decide on colours and specification to make the car really bespoke, then they are given a guided tour around the factory, imbibing the experience and learning what Bugatti is really all about. Then once they have finalised their personal specification, it's time to complete the order. At that point, they need to put down a sizable deposit, and then [varying] increments until the full balance is paid before the car is put into production.' Jeremy would not be drawn on the first deposit required but other sources suggest this is in the region of £300,000.

It's hard to walk down the street without coming across an advert for a car loan. But presumably Veyron buyers always pay cash? Not necessarily so, according to Jeremy. 'People do finance Bugatti Veyrons. But it's all relative. Financing a Lamborghini Gallardo might cost, say £1500 a month; but that's

Afzal Kahn owns two Veyrons, one of which is arguably the most valuable Bugatti in the world. The car carries the number plate 'F1' which is possibly the most expensive registration mark ever. Sources suggest Kahn has been offered between £5 and £10 million for the car, complete with the plate. Kahn is the founder of A Kahn Design Limited which he describes as 'designing and building new vehicles for the rich and famous'. Kahn is considered one of England's most pioneering and successful entrepreneurs and his company is one of only a select few remaining global automotive brands in the UK.

what a lot of people earn in a month. If someone owns a Ford Fiesta that is worth £500, they would think that £1500 a month is completely excessive and why would you go and spend that money on a car? If it's a Veyron, we can put you in touch with a very good finance company. Potentially, you could be looking at paying £20,000–£30,000 a month for a Bugatti. With maybe a deposit of around £250,000 with an end payment too, say £200,000 balloon, it all depends how you structure it.'

Buying a Veyron is not, in Jeremy's opinion, a financial decision anyway: 'When people come here, I say there is no logic switch, why would you come and buy one of these cars? Most supercars will depreciate … but they are a passion and are perceived like a piece of art.'

And why is the Veyron cordoned off, even among such lofty company? 'It's the car that generates the most interest and also the one that is generally seen on the roads the least. It's not that I think people are going to damage it, but if the car is continually being touched and has fingerprints all over it, it would continually need detailing. Again, there is liability of anything unthinkable happening as far as actual accidental damage to one of the cars.'

So I want the Veyron but I haven't got much cash deposit. Would you take a PX? 'There's not many cars that will contribute a reasonable chunk towards a Veyron. It can cause more of an issue because the part-exchange will more than likely be of a relatively high value [but there] can typically be a difference of opinions on a car's value – the client can think their current car is worth more money than you are offering, naturally, so there's often a disparity. With a Veyron they might want to potentially put in more than one car so therefore there's more than one disparity. Most of the time these people are car collectors and want to keep their other cars. Plus they usually have the money to buy the car. They don't tend to swap their old car for their new car.'

Notably, one Bugatti owner in America did exactly the opposite of that and took in a Veyron *as his part-exchange*. His car of choice to PX the £1 million red-and-black, 20,000-mile Bugatti with? A $50,000 Corvette! At the reverse end of the spectrum, another Veyron owner sold his Bugatti complete with a Mercedes-Benz Atego transporter painted to match.

Once again what comes across talking to Jeremy is a *passion* for the car. Sure, he's a salesman and it's his job to make the car look its best. But there's something more, something intangible, it's that celebrity again. 'I think the Veyron is on a pedestal really. No one can knowledgeably argue that it is the same as another car. What is it the same as? Interestingly, if you speak to any technicians who work on these sorts of cars and *know* about these cars, i.e. they are not salesmen, they will tell you that there is no car built like this car. There is no other car that can compare, sure there are some fantastic fast cars: the

LP670, the Enzo, the Carrera GT. However these are more akin to race cars. Amazing cars, I love them, but they are not the same as the Veyron.'

So you've made it to Molsheim to visit the factory; what exactly does a test drive – the one you never asked for, remember? – in a Bugatti Veyron consist of? You are taken out by Pierre-Henri Raphanel, the brand's official test driver and the world record holder as we have seen. 'Most of the test drives are on public roads,' he told me. 'I explain the car first and then I will drive for some time. You have to be aware of the customer, they are very powerful people, most of the time they are leaders, but if I do not lead the test drive, we will both suffer, this car is Formula 1 on the road.'

This is an observation that also applies to journalists reviewing the car: '[On one occasion] we gave a car to a journalist and a photographer together and by the time they came back they had destroyed one gearbox, doing launch control without the button etc., and then there was a big argument because they never accepted what they had done. But we have the telemetry system, even when you switch off the key the satellite gives us readings, so there is no way you can say you didn't do something. We know. From then on, we made a decision to never again give a car to someone alone.'

Pierre will sometimes take a camera and if a customer is driving too fast, he takes a picture of them. 'If I do that, anyone in the world will slow down, it just happens, it has to be safe.' Pierre has one particular trick that appears superficially insane but actually helps him make the test drive more controlled. The purpose of this trick is as much to secure respect and discourage dangerous driving ('sometimes you think we are going to die'), and Pierre finds this trick ultimately helps him keep both people in the cabin safe. So what does he do?

'I try to make them relax for a short while, everyone who goes in this car gets a little bit stressed at first, it is 1001bhp after all. Then I demonstrate the car in a very short stretch of a particular road near Molsheim which has a straight then a big corner. It's maybe ten seconds to demonstrate power, cornering and then braking. At the start of the straight, I will put full power in first gear – full throttle – but only holding the steering wheel with two fingers. The car goes through the gears and is doing 200km/h in a few seconds, but I still only have my two fingers on the steering.

'Then we take the corner on what is a very bumpy road, but still with just the two fingers, all the way through the corner. Then after the car hits 200km/h and we have come out of the corner I hit the brakes . . .'

'And as you hit 200,' I asked, 'and slam the anchors on, that's when you put all your fingers back on the steering wheel . . . ?'

'No! That's when I take my hands *off* the steering wheel.'

I didn't tell him that when I drove the Super Sport my fingers ached for two days because I'd gripped the wheel so hard.

Pierre Henri continued: 'Then I realised that people were so focused on the speed that they were not noticing that I had taken my hands off the wheel. Their brain is getting too much information all at once and it cannot compute it all at the same time. So I had to change the trick.'

'And exactly how did you do that?'

'Now when I brake at 200km/h, I take my hands off and clap. They usually notice that.'

So you've taken delivery of your Bugatti Veyron. As an owner, what is in store for you? How much will it cost to run? What is it like to actually have one of these celebrities in your garage? Well, you've probably guessed that the running costs aren't exactly modest. A standard service is in the region of £12,000. Bugatti recommends an oil change every 12,400 miles but they also prefer a spark-plug change at 37,000 miles. Due to the nature of the car's complex construction, most of the bodywork behind the doors has to come off for this, as well as the intercoolers, so don't even ask how much that will cost. The tyres will set you back about £18,000 and will only last for approximately 6250 miles – if you drive carefully. The wheels need changing with every third set of tyres which will set you back over £35,000. And if you're too heavy on the brakes, a full replacement of front and rear brake pads and discs will cost over £11,000.

When the topic comes to the costs of spare parts, Bugatti's PR director Emanuela Wilm becomes protective of her 'baby'. 'This car is tailor-made, it is not mass market. If you buy a Dior couture dress for €13,000, a spare button costs you probably a hundred times more than one for a high-street dress. Do people talk about it? No! Do people complain about it? No!' And by way of example, she referred me to a notorious incident when a $50 million Picasso painting was accidentally damaged by the owner's elbow. 'The costs for Picasso to paint it were certainly lower than for us to build the Veyron, but the costs for this man to have his painting restored were probably much higher than the costs for repairing a Veyron involved in an accident. The Veyron has been described by many customers as a piece of art on wheels. When restoring a piece of art you would not ask, "What does the canvas cost? The paint? The frame?" You would want it restored the best possible way. Veyron owners look at it the same way.'

You've probably also guessed that the fuel consumption isn't about to get the Green Party dancing for joy, with the 'average' of around 12–14mpg reducing to that figure of less than 3mpg at top speeds. One magazine equated the running costs to at least £5–7 per mile. And what about insurance? For the purposes of this book, the author successfully obtained a quote for a Bugatti, and if you drive like a nun and have never had a speeding ticket of any description, it would set you back just over £25,000 a year. On first glance that sounds exorbitant, but if you were to buy a £10,000 VW Golf, you'd probably expect to pay around £250 insurance, so it's all relative. Given that a replacement fender on a Veyron costs £5500, this quote doesn't actually leave much room for error on the insurer's part. If someone splits your front bumper and isn't insured, to replace that and the Bugatti badge and grille will set you back £16,000. There are actually very few Veyron accidents to research, with Bugatti themselves only being aware of five, but one insurance expert I spoke to said that even a semi-serious shunt in a Veyron would probably generate several hundred thousand pounds' worth of repairs. Even if you get in awkwardly and snap the indicator stalk, it will set you back £4500.

The really frightening figures are reserved for major mechanical malfunctions. Although it's never been required to date, if you somehow 'break' your Veyron's engine, just buying the replacement only – without allowing for any labour – will cost you £225,000. If you mash the gearbox, write out a cheque for £85,000; if it's 'just' the clutch you only need a paltry £30,000 (but please note Bugatti have never had to change any of these parts).

We've already seen that the Veyron is remarkably reliable for such an expensive and powerful car. One reason for this is the extensive testing in development that Dr Schreiber had told me about. Another obvious help is the system they have placed in each car that senses when or if a fault may be about to occur and alerts Bugatti via satellite signal. The Veyron has twenty-seven major on-board computer systems and in the unlikely event of a problem, each ECU has an emergency software program to prevent the car from stopping too suddenly. For example, if the oil pressure drops too low, the engine will automatically lower the rpm. Or if you can't get 98-octane fuel, the engine will automatically retune itself to the octane you did put in. So at high speeds the car will not suddenly lurch to a halt; instead the car's power is reduced and warning lights illuminated. By the time you phone Bugatti about the issue, they will already know about it.

So if you own a Veyron, you can perhaps expect a phone call out of the blue one morning telling you that your tyre pressures are a little low. Part of the reason for this was that many Veyron owners will not use their car too often, some perhaps only in their summer home in southern France for example, and Bugatti wanted to make sure that when they finally came to switch the car on after several months of not being used, that it was ready, willing and able.

Of course, even in a Bugatti Veyron, parts sometimes fail . . . although not as often as you might think, as Dr Schreiber explains: 'We have a very low complaint rate, really very low. We've had very few faults from the beginning of the project. For each car we had to calculate and allow for a certain amount of money for repairs and customer complaints especially in the warranty time, not least because this car is completely new and totally different from anything else on the market; however, now we know that the number of faults and complaints has turned out to be very much lower than we expected.'

Looking at those repair costs, even the super-wealthy will perhaps be tempted to buy Bugatti's extended warranty, over and above the usual cover provided on the original purchase (the Veyron and Grand Sport come with a two-year or 50,000km warranty, while the Super Sport comes with a three-year or 75,000km warranty). This isn't exactly an extended warranty that you might buy from the RAC. The cover guarantees the mechanical and electrical components, as well as the body and paintwork, including a guarantee against rust. The complex computer software will alert the driver to any possible problem and Bugatti will spring into action – even providing the delivery of replacement parts anywhere in the world.

If the Veyron actually breaks down, Bugatti picks up the car, ships it to the nearest official repair shop or dealership and also escorts the driver to their destination. Notably, a 'replacement vehicle' is provided, in this case an Audi A8! Much of this replicates more standard car warranties, but this is not where Bugatti stop. They also issue a so-called 'anti-inconvenience' cheque that 'can be used to cover any expenses resulting from a breakdown, such as hotel accommodation or travel tickets, without any need to produce receipts. A special helpline is available twenty-four hours a day, seven days a week, and all calls are managed personally by a member of Bugatti customer service'. The price? £35,000 for two years. For those of you who are in the market for buying a pre-owned Veyron, a two-year warranty on a used car (if the manufacturer's warranty has expired) costs about £40,000, provided the car is from an official dealership and has been checked first.

Everyday maintenance might cost more than you think too. Once you own the car, you'll probably not want to take it through the 'Superwax' at your local supermarket. You can wash it yourself or, as is perhaps more likely, get one particular US firm to apply a $12,000 tub of wax in a total valet that costs in the region of $20,000.

At Molsheim I'd met the two men in charge of this after-sales service, Manfred Behrend and Frederic Stocks. They explained with great pride how they would look after my Veyron in the event of a rare mechanical failure and it was clear that my every whim would be catered for. One aspect they told me about which easily trumps the rental car option I'd failed so abysmally to exploit was their own unique driving experience, called 'Feeling the Road'. The invited owner spends an entire day with the official test driver Pierre-Henri Raphanel using a demonstrator vehicle good for 300 kilometres of driving. This includes one-to-one tuition on such skills as acceleration, emergency braking, skid control and so on, using a variety of surfaces including an artificial rain system. After this the owner will join Pierre-Henri at the Anneau du Rhin track in Colmar, near to some of France's most luxurious vineyards, where he will have the exclusive use of the circuit. The day is rounded off by moving the car to the larger of the circuit's two tracks where a full-speed session will be undertaken. Then it's off to a beautiful restaurant for dinner with Pierre-Henri to talk about the drive. The experience is offered 'on a strictly individual basis' and costs around $12,000. Another fantastic day offered to Veyron owners is a top-speed outing. Only a select few are invited to the top-secret Ehra-Lessien testing facility near Wolfsburg with ambitions of joining one of the most exclusive speed clubs in the world – those who have driven over 400km/h.

Remember, these are just the running costs. This is after you've already paid for the car – and the amounts some fans of this particular celebrity are willing to part with are staggering. For example, the international success of the Veyron is despite the sometimes punitive import duties which the car attracts. In America, where nearly one-third of all Veyrons reside, there is a 'destination charge' totalling $110,000. When you collect your machine, there's an additional $7000 'guzzler' tax. Further, the Veyron is one of the few cars sold in America in euros, which means that if you decided to order on a Tuesday instead of Monday and the dollar falls by one cent at the foreign exchange in the meantime, the car will cost you an extra £16,000.

Worse still is India, where a 110 per cent import duty operates, which did not stop the first Indian customer buying a Grand Sport at more than double its cost, making the total price an unbelievable $3.6 million. Same goes for China.

The fact that you can buy ten Ferrari 458s for the same price as a Super Sport cannot matter to you if you are thinking of buying a Veyron. One customer spent an extra £50,000 on custom leather. One-off paint jobs are a popular add-on, with one customer reported to have spent nearly half a million dollars – or the price of a Rolls-Royce – on special livery. Another customer was reported to have had certain 'fruity' words illuminated along the door sill. A more conservative optional extra would be your own initials on the petrol cap instead of the famous 'EB'. A 'stone chip guard' costs about £5000 and there are a number of customer wheels for around £35,000 a set.

For all the lofty monetary figures bandied about with the Veyron, in fact in the context of how the ultra-wealthy spend their fortunes, the car is not actually that expensive, relatively speaking. Compared to some of the super-rich's toys, a Bugatti Veyron is in fact quite affordable. Take that bastion of ultra-wealth, for example, the private yacht. One yacht-owning celebrity that I spoke to told me that there are two really memorable days when buying a super-yacht: the day you pick it up and the day you sell it.

BUGATTI VEYRON – A QUEST FOR PERFECTION

Eric Gallina, editor of *Car Design News*: 'It's the first vehicle of its kind to show off the various elements in the two-tone body colour. A car's colours go a long way to communicating a level of prestige and other cars have not executed this as well as on the Veyron. The blend of materials and the detail that is repeated throughout the car adds to this and give it a real sense of occasion that is unique.' His magazine awarded the car its highly prestigious 'Car Design of the Year'.

Finally, with regards to those dazzling Veyron running costs, my particular favourite is a new set of windscreen wipers: £836.

So it's clear that you have to have a fairly bulging bank account to buy and maintain a Bugatti Veyron, let's not pretend otherwise. The worst financial crisis since the Great Depression was a full three years away when Bugatti launched the Veyron to the media in 2005. Even so, such highly priced cars will always elicit gasps of horror from furrowed puritanical brows, amidst mumblings of obscene wealth and inappropriate overspending. Of course, that is nonsense, no more absurd than telling a plumber that he can't and shouldn't own his Nissan GTR. But it does raise an intriguing question: just who owns a car like the Bugatti Veyron?

Notably, Bugatti are fiercely protective of their customers' privacy – in some nations, driving in a car of that value makes you a kidnap risk. They declined to tell me anything about any customers at all, save for the fact that most are businessmen – rather than celebrities – and are usually entrepreneurs who have

made a fortune from an innovative idea. Very few buyers are female, apart from the wife of former VW chairman Ferdinand Piëch, who owns chassis number 7.

There are rumoured to be a number of celebrity owners too, although again it is difficult to verify: Simon Cowell owns a black-on-black model (said to reside in a black-marble floored garage); the New England Patriots quarterback Tom Brady, Premier-League footballer Tim Cahill and former F1 world champion Jensen Button are all sports stars who've owned a Bugatti; film and entertainment stars such as Tom Cruise, hip-hop producer Scott Storch and, of course, Jay-Z are all also rumoured to be Veyron owners. Prodigious car collector Jay Leno is said to have one. In the world of fashion, fellow car collector Ralph Lauren is a Veyron owner too, as is reportedly Nigo, a famous Japanese fashion designer who owns a pink car. US chat show host Conan O'Brien dressed a Veyron up as a mouse as a gag on his programme, although it seems unlikely he drives this actual 'limited edition'.

Away from celebrities owning this celebrity, less high-profile individuals make up the bulk of Veyron customers. Notably there are many multiple buyers

BUGATTI VEYRON

of Veyrons, namely customers with more than one version; again Bugatti would not reveal any details except that one particular owner has 'less than ten'. There is rumoured to be a man in Holland who has three, one in each colour of the Dutch flag; another story suggests a man in the Middle East has turned a Veyron into a water feature/fountain inside his vast private residence. My own personal favourite is the English entrepreneur who has a standard 16.4 with a very early chassis number, a Pur Sang limited edition and the mythical World Record Edition Super Sport, a surely unrivalled combination.

So, having seen a cross-section of the sort of people who own a Veyron, the next question is, what is it actually like to own one? Former investment banker and now professional investor Arne Fredly lives in Monaco and drives a 16.4 in black and red. He has owned or driven many Ferraris, a McLaren SLR, a Porsche Carrera GT, a Koenigsegg, various Lamborghinis and other supercars; he even owns Michael Schumacher's F1 car from 2005 too, so he knows his fast cars and any comparisons are clearly very informed. 'I actually ordered a Veyron after seeing an early prototype at Geneva with eighteen cylinders. I thought, *That's the car for me!* This car was so out of the ordinary, remember this was 1999, before the Enzo even, it was out of this world, just incredible.' Mr Fredly was one of the very first few to put his name down for a Veyron; however, he temporarily took his name off the list when the development of the Veyron suffered those high-profile glitches but by the eventual launch he was eagerly awaiting delivery.

His day-to-day use of the car around the principality confirms the 'easy-to-use' approach works. 'I use it around Monaco, trips to St Tropez, things like that. You can go to the shops if you want to, absolutely, although the only problem is the car has such a high value and you might find yourself in a narrow street with a £500 scooter crashing into you. If it was any wider it would be beyond the limit of practicality, for me a car has to be *useable*. My Lamborghini was harder to park in public car parks. Not so the Veyron.'

He also agrees the car has a celebrity appeal: 'If I take it out tonight, over ten years since the concept cars, remember, people will look. And everyone knows the name of the car, even the girls! When I park outside the casino, people always look and then I've noticed that afterwards when I get home there are always lots of fingerprints all over it! I look after it very well though; I've done a lot of miles but it still looks like new. When I drive to a restaurant in Monaco or use valet parking somewhere, you get a lot of attention, it's so wide and impressive, powerful, it looks so different from anything else. You see a lot of cars in Monaco, multimillion-pound vintage Ferraris and so on, but if people see the Veyron, they go crazy. There's no other car that gets such attention here.' Every Veyron owner in the world will tell you the same.

Mr Fredly once drove his Veyron from Norway to Monaco, a distance of over 2000 kilometres! On another Autobahn trip, a Superbike tried to race him but at 285km/h he saw the bike in his rear-view mirror 'wobbling away' in the slipstream before falling back as the Veyron accelerated again.

He also thinks the car's initial limited offering of colour combinations was missing a trick: 'My Veyron is black and red, a more aggressive look. For me, the car carries lots of combinations of colour very well; you can't really have a bright green Ferrari, for example! And Lambos you can have in crazy colours but not others. For the Bugatti, there are so many combinations that work.'

And are there any negatives? 'Not really, no. The only problem I have with it is the cost of tyres. If they were cheaper I would use the car every day. The tyre costs can be many times the service cost if you use it for say 10,000 kilometres a year. I can afford the tyres but I am a businessman, I don't like to waste money.'

Mr Fredly calls the car a 'cruiser': 'I've had many supercars but I've never had such a feeling of quality and also safety at high speed. I've tried to sum that car up and I usually say, "When you drive the car it feels like it was made to do 500km/h but it *only* goes 408." That's the Bugatti for me. For what it is, there is nothing to compare, it is unbelievable.'

For those of you reading this for whom the Veyron will always remain an elusive dream – and let's be honest, that's the vast majority of us – take solace in this fact. On the day I'd tested the Super Sport with Dr Schreiber, you may recall he told me proudly of his new 'baby', the chunky and robust-looking VW Amarok pick-up truck. The following day, as I walked into Hannover airport to check in, I went to find the gate for my flight. As I did I noticed a show car parked near to a newsagents. The silhouette looked familiar so I walked over to see what it was and was charmed to find it was a VW Amarok, Dr Schreiber's 'new baby'. I smiled secretly to myself, knowing that this light commercial vehicle standing here on display in the Departures building had just a little Bugatti stardust sprinkled over its DNA. And I also knew that the process of the Veyron's genius filtering down into other cars within the group and then out into the wider car world had already started. If you own a VW Amarok, then know that you are a lot closer to owning a Bugatti Veyron than you might otherwise think . . . and as a result, soon we might all be too.

AFTERWORD

Sitting in Casino Square in Monaco is perhaps the ultimate exercise in people watching. The wealth and extravagance hangs in the air, the clement weather exaggerates the undeniable beauty of the architecture and the whole experience is soundtracked by an almost constant stream of supercar engines. Even from the fifth floor of a hotel, it's apparent when a Ferrari or Lamborghini is pulling up. A quick look over the balcony confirms whether it's a 458 or 360, swiftly followed by a Murcielago or perhaps a Gallardo. Monaco is one of the few places in the world where you get to hear supercars as much as see them.

There is a certain draw to Monaco for any writer working on a book about hypercar performance and ultra-wealth. For Bugatti too, there is a historical link; Bugatti has numerous ties with the principality. One of its most revered drivers, Louis Chiron (after whom the 18/4 concept car was named), was born there in 1899 and even operated a car dealership just down the coast in Nice; similarly the marque would often race well in Monte Carlo's grand prix. The Veyron itself had been showcased here too prior to its launch, on that gruelling world tour of blue-riband social and automotive events. The facade of the famous Casino was even been painted in Bugatti's blue and red company colours. This unique principality is perhaps the Veyron's most natural habitat.

But away from the glitz, the money and the splendour, just a few miles along the Côte d'Azur lies a sleepy and ancient village called Eze, perched 1400 feet above sea level on a rocky outcrop, huddled around a twelfth-century castle. This is where Pierre Veyron, the Bugatti race driver who lends his name to this most inspiring of celebrities, finally passed away in 1970, aged sixty-seven. He'd moved here after retirement, a typically understated choice of location for the Indian summer of a dashing and inspirational racing driver. When Pierre Veyron died, the Bugatti brand was inactive. Likewise, at that time, only a select few Bugatti purists and motorsport historians would readily recognise his name and achievements. What would he have thought had he known his former employer christened arguably their greatest ever creation after him? Veyron was so intimately involved with the Le Mans-winning race car that paradoxically proved to be Bugatti's desperate nadir with the premature death of Ettore's son Jean; how fitting that more than a quarter of a century after his death, this great driver was also the inspiration behind the brand's rebirth. His journey ended here, my quest has to also. And so ends the true and faithful history of the Bugatti Veyron of Molsheim.

Despite my early problems, I'd eventually met the celebrity I was so fascinated by. In my line of work, there's an old adage 'Don't meet your heroes' for fear of disappointment; I ignored that but there had been no disappointment. Just confirmation that the Veyron is, after all, a celebrity, out of the ordinary, something . . . special. The Veyron does indeed tick all the 'celebrity' boxes.

I am aware that mine is a partisan tale but I also know the difference between a windmill and a giant. Of course, there will be some (press and public alike) who do not see the Veyron as a celebrity, who do not 'get' its emotion. But this book has never been about reviews or expert critique. It is the story of a very post-modern celebrity and my experience chasing the fastest car ever built. And how can that ever be anything other than emotional?

Coming back to an earlier premise, a very surprising and pleasant part of this quest has been the people. Bugatti itself obviously has the image of a highly prestigious global brand; it is exactly that, but my own experience also tells me at its very heart it is a boutique brand, a very small cluster of passionate, close-knit people working long hours every day. This is something I often see behind the scenes of many huge celebrities. Of course, I know VW are hiding behind the curtains side of stage, just as major record labels are often found lurking behind many 'independent' artists, but in both cases the achievement is no less for that fact. And those characters, those individual personalities whom I'd met on my travels that have steeped themselves deep in the history of this creative brand, they have an accumulative potency that is beguiling and disproportionate – because on a daily basis, the Veyron is even greater than the sum of these voices.

Had they achieved Dr Piëch's original goals? The statistics tell us that with those famous three performance targets they had unequivocally succeeded. As for the fourth, more problematic aim, the one that must have kept Dr Schreiber awake at night, it was hard to argue that the Veyron was not easy to drive to the opera.

'Crawling' up the M40 motorway one final time on the way home from my quest, my eye frequently flicked to the speedo, just as it did that day in the Super Sport, except here the needle was drifting innocuously between 70 and 80mph. I recalled that traffic jam on the Autobahn and how, as we edged our way towards Wolfsburg I had, if only momentarily, forgotten that I was driving a car costing seven figures. Yet that was only thirty minutes after I'd topped 300km/h. In the context of this English motorway, it's hard to comprehend what 190mph felt like.

In a sense, it doesn't matter, what is crucial is the recognition that the Veyron is a *complete* package: Form, Technique, Function.

I'd set out on a quest to chase perfection; VW had set out on their own quest to create perfection. So is the Bugatti Veyron perfect? Maybe, maybe not. It's a question that will probably never be answered to everyone's satisfaction, but it's been an amazing journey trying to find out.

What the Bugatti team have achieved with the Veyron is a rare blend of mechanics and passion; it is hard, of course, to not be in awe of the engineering achievement, the bare statistics alone will always dazzle. But looking back on my travels, the conversations I recall most vividly with acutely expansive minds such as Dr Schreiber and Dr Paefgen are the ones peppered with words such as 'feel', 'passion' and 'emotion'. Question of science and progress or matters of the heart?

Driving back from the airport in the cold light of a wet English spring afternoon, my mind couldn't help but be thrown back once again to the brand's founder, that enigmatic, some even say eccentric boy who'd first made tricycles in Milan. 'If Ettore had seen what has happened,' Bugatti brand historian Julius Kruta had told me as we'd wandered around the Atelier in Molsheim, 'he would be very happy. He had a big ego, so his name is still there while the names of the other guys he knew, characters from the distant past like Dalage, Voison and Jano, these were his friends but they are all gone, only very few people remember them. Ettore would be very proud that his name is still shining. And besides, if he'd seen the Veyron, I think he would have been speechless.'

Of course, this particular knight-errant was never going to return home with the object of the quest tucked furtively under his arm in a worn leather satchel; this was always more Sir Galahad than Indy, even though this book's path is glittered with more gold than Jason's mythical fleece. This matters not one iota. I'd driven the Bugatti Veyron. For a few gloriously vicarious moments, I'd inhabited the world of this celebrity.

And I'd learned that, even if only sometimes, nothing is impossible.

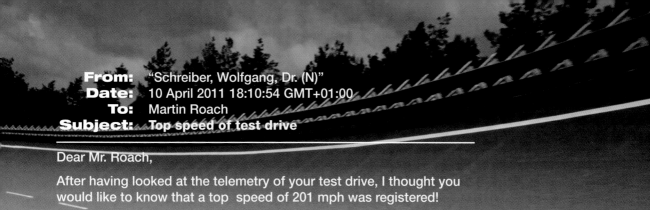

From: "Schreiber, Wolfgang, Dr. (N)"
Date: 10 April 2011 18:10:54 GMT+01:00
To: Martin Roach
Subject: Top speed of test drive

Dear Mr. Roach,

After having looked at the telemetry of your test drive, I thought you would like to know that a top speed of 201 mph was registered!

Fast, very fast . . .

Regards, Wolfgang Schreiber

Acknowledgements

This book is dedicated to Dr Kerry Spackman … *Thank you.*

A *very* special and sincere thank you to Emanuela Wilm who has been an extraordinary help with this project and despite always being exceptionally busy, never *once* failed to return my calls, emails and texts. Without her enormous assistance, this quest might just have proved impossible. Thank you.

To Dr Wolfgang Schreiber: certain experiences in life you take to the grave. I thought driving at 200mph+ on a public road would take *me* to my grave. Thanks to the stunning car you engineered, I enjoyed one of the greatest days of my life (shame on you for upstaging Santa). It was an absolute pleasure to meet you and my 'Afternoon with the Doctor' is something I will never forget.

Thanks also to the capaciously intelligent Julius Kruta who has made me reconsider the definition of 'brand expert'; thank you for your time, expertise and good humour.

Thanks to Dr Paefgen, who found time for me in his hectic schedule and filled an afternoon with enough fascinating stories for a whole book.

Thanks to the following people who also interviewed so brilliantly for the book: Fred Schulemann, Pierre Raphanel, Manfred Behrend, Frederic Stocks, Jeremy Mitchell and HR Owen, Arne Fredly, Eric Gallina and *Car Design News*.

Thanks to Christina Lange and Christiane Schwindack for fielding all my emails and being so incredibly helpful; thanks for the technical information and a lift home to Klaudia Labersweiler (aka Super Mum); thanks to Paul Riches for his amazing tour. And, of course, a special thank you to everyone at Bugatti who helped me on my quest.

Thanks also to: Dr Ulrich Eichorn for taking the call and making such an effort for me; Peter Ward, Dave Clarke and DPC Media, Trevor Horwood, Jeremy Hart, Liam Howlett, Jon Bentley, Afzal Kahn, David Coulthard, Surjit Singh Rai, Kjetil Sviland, Jörg Knoblich, Carl Beebee and Ant Davies at 12.42 Films.

Thanks to Trevor Dolby, a genuine maverick and a one-off, someone who fiercely values books above spreadsheets. Thanks for taking a punt on me and my ridiculous idea, Trev.

Thanks to my editor at Preface, Nicola Taplin, who made the process of working on this book an absolute pleasure as she always does, even under very demanding circumstances for us both.

The excellent National Geographic documentary on the Veyron is highly recommended; the programme was directed and edited by Dylan Weiss and the Executive Producer/Writer was Milt Weiss.

Finally, special thanks to my wonderful wife Kaye, for putting up with three boys talking about cars.

For full technical data on every Bugatti Veyron model, as well as extensive historical information and a huge brand archive, please visit: www.bugatti.com

Author's Note: Martin Roach would like to point out that at no point did Bugatti demand or even request copy approval; likewise no reassurance or guarantee was given to anyone collaborating in this book about its contents.

This book was sound-tracked by Arcade Fire's *The Suburbs*, The Streets' *Computers And Blues* and My Chemical Romance's *Danger Days: The True Lives Of The Fabulous Killjoys*.

About the Author:
Martin Roach is a Number 1 best-selling ghostwriter and author with many books on music, celebrity, sport and youth culture to his name. He gained a degree in Historical Research before writing his first book aged 21 – he has since sold over 1.5 million copies of his works. He can be contacted at: www. bestsellingghostwriter.com

THE VEYRON PROJECT TEAM

The following is a list of the Bugatti personnel who worked on the Veyron project.

Adler, Jens
Ahrends, Uwe
Amler, Klaus
Anastasio, Joanna
Anscheidt, Achim
Bahr, Hans-Michael
Bäker, Wolfgang
Beck, Nelli
Beneke, Lars
Biccochi, Loris
Block, Andreas
Blumenstein, Friedrich
Blyszcz, Norbert
Bock, Christian
Bode, Michael
Böttger, Ralph
Brunetti, Gian Carlo
Bscher Dr, Thomas
Buss, Jens-Gerold
Bussat, Sven-Holger
Busse, Thomas
Dannies, Imre
David, Arnaud
Deuschle, Dana
Domschitz, Jochen
Eckhardt, Steffen
Eichler, Torsten
Ene, Eduard
Eschwey, Denis
Fabig, Stephan
Fiedler, Jülf
Figas, Andreas
Finkbeiner, Albert
Fischer, Holger
Fischer, Lars
Fürstenberg, Tilo
Geffers, Frank
Gehendges, Sven
George, Thomas
Gericke, Michael
Gerloff, Martin
Geyer, Christoph
Giese, Steven
Götzke, Frank

Greite, Carmen
Gries, Gregor
Gronert, Bernd
Grumer, Jörg
Gütte, Maik
Hammer, Gerd
Hartauer, Uwe
Haschke, Simone
Hasselmeyer, Alfred
Hecht, Hendrik
Heine, Marco
Heling, Christian
Hennicke, Andreas
Henschelmann, Markus
Heßler, Olaf
Heyl, Frank
Hinze, Dirk
Hoffmann, Louisa
Hohlstein, Günther
Ingwerth, Thomas
Jahn, Sara
Janssen, Susanne
Jobst, Andrea
Juwick, Frank
Kalis-Cloer, Dirk
Kassel, Sophie
Keil, Dirk
Kin, Nathalia
Kislat, Michael
Kleinau, Jens
Kludt, Alexander
Klum, Christian
Knötig, Tobias
Kodra, Michael
Kolbe, Olaf
Krause, Swen
Kullig, André
Kumpan, Dimitri
Kurowski, Andreas
Labersweiler, Klaudia
Lamp, Georg
Lamp, Reinhard
Lange, Ingo
Lechner, Reinhard

Leinz, Robert
Lo Bianco, Nadine
Lopez, Mario
Lovre, Tanja
Lüder, Jens
Lutz, Wolf-Rüdiger
Marek, Norbert
Minuth, Marius
Misdorf, Winfried
Monni, Luigi
Mrácek, Steffi
Müller, Heiko
Müller, Philipp
Neumann Dr, Karl-Heinz
Neumann, Stephen
Nielsen, Lars
Osburg, Michael
Osterloh, Sascha
Otte, Jürgen
Pagel, Heinz-Dieter
Parlow, Günter
Peters, Frank
Pflug, Meike
Pietruschka, Georg-Anton
Pollok, Richard
Preuß, Andreas
Purps, Sarah
Rahlfs, Siegfried
Reinosch, Jörg
Riedel, Alexander
Riffel, Jörg
Rigl, Wolfgang
Rommelfanger, Pierre
Ryl, Frank
Sallmann, Henny
Salomon, Etienne
Saluzzi, Vincenzo
Schadikin, Elena
Schäfer, Andreas
Scheibel, Markus
Schirmer, Miriam
Schmechta, Leo
Schneider, Holger
Schnell, Hartmut

Scholle, Toralf
Schreiber, Markus
Schreiber, Dr Wolfgang
Schrieber, Nicole
Schulenburg, Jens
Schulze, Uwe
Schwarzer, Paul
Sievers, Ulrich
Slopianka, Siegbert
Sorighe, Sandra
Spakman, Derk Jan
Sprenger, Helmut
Sprung, Heiko
Stäblein, Volker
Starmann, Daniel
Stehncken, Christoph
Streilein, Oliver
Tasler, Patricia
Thomas, Verena
Tutzer, Peter
Twardowski, Tilo
Umbach, Florian
Urban, Detlef
Von der Ohe, Christian
Wachtel, Jens
Walczak, Knut
Wanke, Maik
Warda, Rüdiger
Weber, Frank
Wehren, Volker
Weidemann, Fabian
Weiß, Christian
Weiss, Steffen
Wessels, Jan
Wetzel, Christian
Wiese, Klaus
Wittekop, Christian
Wittekop, Ulrich
Wucherpfennig, Robert
Zehaluk, Herbert
Ziebart, Jutta
Zygmanowski, Manuel